RENAL DIET COC FOR BEGINNERS

Quick and Easy Delicious Recipes Low in Sodium, Phosphorus and Potassium to Manage Your Kidney Disease. Flexible 60-Day Smart Meal Plan Included.

Roger Dash

Table of Contents

Introduction

What is Nephropathy (Kidney Disease)

Diabetic nephropathy, a form of chronic kidney disease (CKD), occurs when the kidneys, responsible for regulating fluid and salt levels in the body and crucial for blood pressure control and cardiovascular health, are affected by high blood sugar levels resulting from diabetes. This condition can be observed in individuals with type 1, type 2, or gestational diabetes, which occurs during pregnancy and increases the risk of type 2 diabetes later in life.

Diabetes disrupts the body's ability to produce or use insulin properly, leading to elevated glucose levels that gradually damage various parts of the body, including the cardiovascular system and kidneys. This kidney damage is specifically referred to as diabetic nephropathy, which serves as a significant cause of long-term kidney disease & end-stage renal disease (ESRD). In ESRD, the kidneys become insufficient to meet daily life requirements, potentially leading to kidney failure with severe consequences.

Nephropathy can affect individuals with any type of diabetes, as it stems from the damage caused by high blood glucose levels. The kidneys, responsible for filtering blood from the body's arteries, are adversely affected by elevated blood glucose levels.

According to a 2016 study, 20-40% of people with diabetes develop some form of kidney disease. Diagnostic tests may reveal the presence of the following indicators:

- High levels of albumin in the urine: Healthy kidneys should not contain any albumin protein in the urine.
- Low glomerular filtration rate (GFR): The kidneys' primary function is to filter blood, and kidney damage impairs this process. Ideally, the kidneys should function at 100% or have a GFR of 100. A GFR of 60% or higher does not indicate kidney disease, while a range of 15-60% is indicative of kidney disease. A GFR below 15% signifies kidney failure.

ESRD represents the final stage of kidney disease, with diabetic nephropathy being the leading cause of ESRD cases in the United States. Approximately 40-50% of ESRD cases are linked to diabetes, necessitating dialysis for individuals with ESRD.

Managing blood sugar levels effectively can reduce the risk of developing diabetic nephropathy. Whether a person has type 1 or type 2 diabetes, they can mitigate the risk by:

- Monitoring and maintaining blood glucose levels within the target range.
- Following a healthy diet low in sugar and salt.
- Engaging in regular exercise.
- Adhering to a prescribed treatment plan, which may involve insulin or other medications.
- Maintaining a healthy weight.

Types of Kidney Disease

Chronic kidney disease (CKD) occurs when the kidneys sustain long-term damage, leading to a decline in their capacity to effectively filter waste and fluid from the bloodstream. The accumulation of waste within the body can have detrimental effects on one's health. As time progresses, the damage to the kidneys and their functionality can deteriorate, eventually resulting in kidney failure or end-stage renal disease, wherein the kidneys cease to function entirely.

Fabry disease is an uncommon hereditary condition characterized by the malfunctioning of various organs in the body, including the heart, brain, and kidneys. It hinders the adequate supply of blood to these organs, potentially resulting in chronic kidney disease or kidney failure.

Cystinosis is a rare disorder where the accumulation of a natural chemical called cystine in the body causes health complications. Kidney damage caused by cystinosis can lead to kidney failure. Individuals with cystinosis must take medication to reduce their cystine levels and may require a kidney transplant. Cystinosis is inherited and is typically diagnosed in infancy.

Glomerulonephritis refers to the impairment and loss of functionality in the tiny filters (glomeruli) within the kidneys responsible for purifying the blood. As a consequence, waste and fluid removal from the blood become compromised, potentially leading to kidney failure. Glomerulonephritis can arise from various health conditions, and treatment depends on the underlying cause.

IgA nephropathy is a disease where proteins produced by the immune system accumulate in the kidneys, causing damage to the glomeruli, the blood-filtering units. The development of this damage is gradual, often unnoticed by individuals affected. Over time, IgA nephropathy can progress to chronic kidney disease, kidney failure, or even death. While there is no cure for IgA nephropathy, medications can slow down kidney damage.

Lupus nephritis is an autoimmune disease characterized by inflammation, pain, and damage throughout the body, including the kidneys. This can result in chronic kidney disease or kidney failure. The exact cause of lupus nephritis is unknown, and it cannot be cured. However, with treatment, many people with lupus can manage symptoms and prevent severe kidney damage.

aHUS (atypical hemolytic uremic syndrome) is an exceedingly rare genetic disease that tends to run in families. It causes the formation of small blood clots within the body's small blood vessels. These clots can obstruct blood flow to the kidneys and other organs, leading to damage. Not all individuals with aHUS experience symptoms, but for those who do, symptoms often manifest after a triggering event, such as pregnancy or cancer.

Polycystic kidney disease (PKD) is an inherited disorder that causes the growth of fluid-filled cysts on the kidneys and other organs. These cysts can diminish the kidney's capacity to filter waste and fluid from the blood. Over time, PKD can progress to kidney failure. While there is no cure for PKD, treatments can slow down cyst growth and mitigate associated health issues.

Various other rare diseases can impair kidney function, reducing their ability to filter waste and fluid from the blood. This damage can result in chronic kidney disease or kidney failure.

Diet for Those Suffering from Nephropathy

A proper diet plays a crucial role in managing nephropathy, a condition that affects kidney function. Here are some dietary recommendations for individuals suffering from nephropathy:

1. **Limit protein intake:** Since the kidneys may have difficulty processing and eliminating waste products from protein metabolism, it is recommended to limit the amount of protein in your diet. Consult a healthcare professional or a registered dietitian to determine the appropriate protein intake for your specific condition.

2. **Control sodium (salt) intake:** Excessive sodium consumption can lead to fluid retention and high blood pressure, which can strain the kidneys. Limit your sodium intake by avoiding processed and packaged foods, restaurant meals, and adding salt to your meals. Instead, use herbs, spices, and other seasonings to enhance the flavor of your food.

3. **Monitor potassium levels:** Some individuals with nephropathy may have high levels of potassium in their blood, which can be harmful to the heart and other organs. Limit potassium-rich foods, such as bananas, oranges, tomatoes, potatoes, and avocado. Your healthcare provider or dietitian can guide you on maintaining a suitable potassium balance.

4. **Manage phosphorus intake:** Impaired kidney function can lead to high levels of phosphorus in the blood, causing bone and heart problems. Restrict phosphorus-rich foods like dairy products, nuts, seeds, chocolate, and carbonated beverages. Consider using phosphorus binders as prescribed by your healthcare provider to help control phosphorus levels.

5. **Watch fluid intake:** Depending on the severity of your kidney function, you may need to restrict fluid intake to avoid fluid overload. This is especially important if you experience swelling (edema) or have difficulty breathing due to fluid retention. Your healthcare provider or dietitian can advise you on the appropriate fluid limits for your condition.

6. **Monitor carbohydrates:** If you have diabetes in addition to nephropathy, it's important to manage your blood sugar levels. Monitor your carbohydrate intake and follow any recommendations provided by your healthcare team to maintain stable blood sugar levels.

7. **Individualize your diet:** It's essential to work with a registered dietitian who specializes in renal nutrition. They can assess your specific needs, consider your medical history, medications, and lab results, and create a personalized meal plan that meets your nutritional requirements while managing nephropathy.

5 Simple Steps to Slow Down Nephropathy

To slow down the progression of nephropathy (kidney damage), it's crucial to take proactive steps to maintain kidney health. Below are 5 simple steps you can follow:

1. Get your blood pressure under control: High blood pressure can worsen kidney damage. Follow a low-sodium diet, engage in regular physical activity, and take prescribed blood pressure medications as directed. Regularly monitor your blood pressure and strive to maintain a healthy range.

2. Manage your blood sugar levels: If you have diabetes, effectively controlling your blood sugar levels is vital. Monitor your blood glucose levels consistently, adhere to your prescribed diabetes management plan, take medications as instructed, and follow a balanced diet that promotes stable blood sugar levels. Keeping your blood sugar within the target range can help prevent or slow down kidney damage.

3. Maintain a healthy weight: Excess weight can strain the kidneys and contribute to the progression of nephropathy. Strive to achieve and sustain a healthy weight by combining regular physical activity with a balanced, portion-controlled diet. Seek guidance from a healthcare professional or registered dietitian to develop a personalized weight management plan that suits your specific needs.

4. Embrace a kidney-friendly diet: Adopt a diet that supports kidney health. This typically involves reducing protein intake, limiting sodium (salt) consumption, managing phosphorus and potassium levels, and monitoring fluid intake, as described in the previous response on the diet for nephropathy. Collaborate with a registered dietitian specializing in renal nutrition to create a customized meal plan that suits your dietary requirements.

5. Stay hydrated and avoid kidney-damaging substances: Maintaining proper hydration is crucial for kidney function and overall well-being. Consult your healthcare provider to determine the appropriate fluid intake for your condition. Additionally, steer clear of substances that can harm the kidneys, such as excessive alcohol, certain medications, and toxins. Follow your healthcare provider's advice regarding medications and exercise caution when using over-the-counter drugs and herbal supplements.

Why Maintain an Adequate Water Balance?

Maintaining an adequate water balance is crucial for overall health and well-being due to several important reasons:

- **Proper hydration:** Water is essential to keep the body properly hydrated, supporting vital functions like digestion, circulation, temperature regulation, and nutrient absorption. It ensures the transport of nutrients and oxygen to cells, the elimination of waste products, and the lubrication of joints and tissues.

- **Kidney function:** The kidneys are responsible for maintaining water balance by filtering waste products and excess fluid from the blood, producing urine, and regulating electrolyte levels. Optimal kidney function depends on sufficient water intake, which promotes efficient filtration and prevents the formation of kidney stones by diluting urine.

- **Fluid balance:** Maintaining the right balance of fluids is critical for optimal body functioning. Throughout the day, the body loses water through activities like sweating, breathing, and urination. Regular water intake replenishes this lost fluid, preserving fluid balance and preventing dehydration and associated health issues such as electrolyte imbalances.
- **Digestion and metabolism:** Water is vital for digestion and metabolism. It aids in the breakdown of food, facilitates nutrient absorption, and supports the elimination of waste through bowel movements. Sufficient water intake promotes a healthy digestive system, prevents constipation, and supports overall gastrointestinal well-being.
- **Physical performance and cognitive function:** Proper hydration is essential for peak physical and mental performance. During physical activity, adequate water intake helps regulate body temperature, maintain adequate blood volume, and support muscle function. Dehydration can lead to reduced exercise performance, fatigue, and impaired cognitive function, affecting concentration, memory, and mental clarity.
- **Skin health:** Well-hydrated skin appears more youthful, elastic, and healthy. Water plays a vital role in maintaining skin moisture and promoting overall skin health and appearance. Inadequate water intake can contribute to dry skin, wrinkles, and various skin-related problems.

What to Eat at The Restaurant

When dining out with nephropathy (kidney disease), it's crucial to make mindful choices that promote kidney health. Here are tips on selecting the right foods:

1. **Go for low-sodium options:** Sodium can worsen kidney damage and high blood pressure. Choose dishes labeled as low-sodium or inquire about low-salt alternatives. Avoid adding extra salt and steer clear of high-sodium foods like processed meats, canned soups, and fried items.
2. **Opt for lean protein:** Protein is important but excessive intake can strain the kidneys. Choose lean protein sources like grilled chicken, fish, or legumes. Avoid high-fat meats, processed meats, and excessive cheese.
3. **Incorporate fruits & vegetables:** Fruits and vegetables are generally kidney-friendly, being low in sodium and rich in nutrients. Opt for fresh or steamed options without added salt or high-sodium sauces. Consider potassium restrictions if advised and choose lower-potassium options when necessary.
4. **Limit phosphorus-rich foods:** If phosphorus intake needs to be managed, restrict foods high in phosphorus such as dairy, nuts, seeds, and processed foods. Inquire about ingredients and preparation methods to make informed choices.
5. **Mind portion sizes:** Restaurant servings are often larger than recommended portions, leading to excessive calorie and nutrient intake. Share a meal or request a half portion. Balance your plate with appropriate amounts of protein, grains, and vegetables.
6. **Exercise caution with sauces and dressings:** Many sauces, dressings, and condiments contain high sodium, phosphorus, and potassium. Request dressings on the side or choose lower-sodium options. Explore alternatives like lemon juice, herbs, or vinegar for added flavor.
7. **Stay hydrated:** Hydrate with water or unsweetened beverages. Avoid sugary drinks, which can contribute to excessive calories and may not be suitable for certain kidney conditions.

Shopping List

What to Eat

A renal diet, also known as a kidney-friendly diet, aims to manage the intake of certain nutrients to support kidney function and minimize the risk of complications. Here are some recommended foods to include in a renal diet:

1. **High-quality protein sources:** Opt for lean proteins such as skinless poultry, fish, eggs, and plant-based protein sources like legumes and tofu. These provide essential amino acids while minimizing the burden on the kidneys.
2. **Low-potassium fruits and vegetables:** Choose fruits and vegetables with lower potassium content, such as apples, berries, grapes, cabbage, cauliflower, green beans, and lettuce. Be cautious with high-potassium fruits like bananas, oranges, and kiwis, and high-potassium vegetables like tomatoes and potatoes.

3. **Low-phosphorus foods:** Limit phosphorus-rich foods and opt for lower-phosphorus alternatives. Examples include fresh fruits, vegetables, white bread, rice, and pasta. Dairy products, nuts, seeds, and processed foods tend to be higher in phosphorus and should be consumed in moderation.

4. **Limited sodium:** Reduce sodium intake by avoiding processed and packaged foods, canned soups, deli meats, and fast food. Instead, choose fresh or homemade meals and use herbs, spices, and other low-sodium seasonings to enhance flavors.

5. **Controlled fluid intake:** Depending on your specific needs, your healthcare provider may recommend monitoring your fluid intake. In general, it's important to stay hydrated but avoid excessive fluid consumption. Follow your healthcare provider's advice on fluid restrictions.

6. **Healthy fats:** Incorporate sources of healthy fats, such as avocados, olive oil, and fatty fish like salmon, which provide omega-3 fatty acids. Limit saturated and trans fats found in fried foods, fatty cuts of meat, and processed snacks.

7. **Limited phosphorus additives:** Be cautious of additives like phosphoric acid, which can be found in colas and some processed foods. These can contribute to higher phosphorus levels in the body.

What to Avoid

On a renal diet, there are certain foods that are generally recommended to be avoided or limited due to their high content of certain nutrients that can potentially burden the kidneys. Here are some foods to avoid or restrict on a renal diet:

1. **High-potassium foods:** Limit or avoid high-potassium foods such as bananas, oranges, kiwis, potatoes, tomatoes, spinach, and avocados. These foods can raise potassium levels in the blood, which can be problematic for individuals with compromised kidney function.

2. **High-phosphorus foods:** Restrict foods rich in phosphorus, including dairy products (milk, cheese, yogurt), nuts, seeds, legumes, whole grains, and processed foods. Excess phosphorus can lead to mineral imbalances and bone problems.

3. **High-sodium foods:** Minimize sodium intake by avoiding processed and packaged foods, canned soups, deli meats, fast food, and salty snacks. High sodium levels can contribute to fluid retention and increased blood pressure.

4. **High-protein foods:** While protein is important, excessive protein intake can put strain on the kidneys. Limit consumption of red meat, organ meats, high-fat meats, and processed meats. Moderation is key, and it's recommended to consult with a dietitian to determine the appropriate protein intake for your individual needs.

5. **Fluids:** Depending on your specific condition, you may need to monitor your fluid intake. Your healthcare provider will advise you on the appropriate amount of fluids to consume. It's important to balance hydration while avoiding excessive fluid retention.

6. **Phosphorus additives:** Watch out for phosphorus additives like phosphoric acid, often found in colas and some processed foods. These additives can contribute to elevated phosphorus levels.

Chapter 1.   Breakfast Recipes

1. Buckwheat Pancakes

Preparation Time: 10 minutes

Cooking Time: 15 minutes

Servings: 2

Ingredients:

- 1/2 large-sized egg
- 1 cup of unsweetened rice milk
- 1/2 cup of buckwheat flour
- 1/2 teaspoon of apple cider vinegar
- 3/4 tablespoon of granulated sugar
- 1/4 cup of all-purpose flour
- 1/2 teaspoon of vanilla extract
- 1/2 teaspoon of baking powder
- 1 tablespoon of butter, divided

Directions:

1. In a small bowl, mix the apple cider vinegar with the rice milk. Allow to sit for five minutes.
2. In a large bowl, sift together the buckwheat flour and all-purpose flour. Add the sugar and baking powder.
3. Combine the rice milk mixture, vanilla extract, and egg with the flour mixture, stirring until you have a smooth batter.
4. Heat 3/4 teaspoon of butter in a large skillet over medium heat. Pour the batter into the skillet using a 1/4 cup measure for each pancake. Cook for 2-3 minutes or until bubbles form on the surface. Flip and cook for another 1-2 minutes.
5. Transfer the cooked pancakes to a serving plate and continue with the remaining batter in batches, adding more butter to the skillet as needed.

Per Serving: Calories: 281kcal; Fat: 0.32oz; Carbs: 1.69oz; Protein: 0.35oz; Sodium: 132mg; Potassium: 0.0105oz; Phosphorus: 0.0041oz

2. Spinach and Mushroom Frittata

Preparation time: 10 minutes

Cooking time: 20 minutes

Servings: 4

Ingredients:

- 6 large eggs
- 1/4 cup skim milk
- 1 cup chopped spinach
- 1 cup sliced mushrooms
- 1/4 cup diced onions
- 1/4 cup shredded low-fat cheddar cheese
- Salt and pepper to taste
- Cooking spray

Directions:

1. Preheat the oven to 350 deg. F.
2. In a bowl, whisk the eggs with skim milk. Season with salt and pepper.
3. Heat an oven-safe skillet over medium heat then coat it with cooking spray.
4. Add the onions and mushrooms to the skillet then sauté for 3-4 minutes until softened.
5. Add the chopped spinach to the skillet then cook for another 2 minutes until wilted.
6. Transfer the beaten eggs over the vegetables in the skillet.
7. Sprinkle the shredded cheese on top of the egg mixture.
8. Transfer the skillet to the preheated oven then bake for 15-20 minutes 'til the frittata is set and slightly golden.
9. Remove from the oven, let it cool for a few minutes, then cut into wedges.
10. Serve warm.

Per serving: Calories: 150kcal; Fat: 0.32oz; Carbs: 0.14oz; Protein: 0.42oz; Sodium: 220mg; Potassium: 0.0092oz; Phosphorus: 0.0063oz

3. Breakfast Burrito with Green Chilies

Preparation time: 10 minutes

Cooking time: 8 minutes

Servings: 2

Ingredients:

- 4 eggs
- ½ teaspoon hot pepper sauce
- 2 tablespoons salsa
- 1 tablespoons of diced green chilies
- ¼ teaspoon of ground cumin
- 2 flour tortillas

Directions:

1. Over medium heat, coat a medium-sized skillet with nonstick cooking spray.
2. In a bowl, combine green chilies, eggs, spicy sauce, and cumin.
3. Once the skillet is heated, pour the egg mixture in, and cook while stirring for one to two minutes or until the egg is set.
4. Toasted tortillas should be heated in another pan or microwave for 20 seconds.
5. Each tortilla should have 1/2 an egg on it before being rolled up burrito-style.
6. Serve with a tablespoon of salsa.

Per serving: Calories: 225kcal; Fat: 0.56oz; Carbs: 0.046oz; Protein: 0.46oz; Sodium: 196mg; Potassium: 0.0069oz; Phosphorus: 0.0043oz

4. Whole Grain Pancakes

Preparation time: 10 minutes

Cooking time: 15 minutes

Servings: 4

Ingredients:

- 1 cup whole wheat flour
- 1 tablespoon sugar
- 1 teaspoon baking powder
- 1/2 teaspoon baking soda
- 1/4 teaspoon salt
- 1 cup skim milk
- 1 large egg
- 1 tablespoon melted butter
- Cooking spray

Directions:

1. In a huge bowl, whisk together the sugar, baking powder, whole wheat flour, baking soda & salt.
2. In a separate bowl, whisk together skim milk, egg, and melted butter.
3. Transfer the wet ingredients in to the dry ingredients then stir until just combined. Do not overmix; the batter can be slightly lumpy.
4. Heat your non-stick skillet or griddle over medium heat then coat it with cooking spray.
5. Pour ¼ cup of batter onto the skillet for each pancake.
6. Cook until bubbles form on the surface, then flip then cook for another 1-2 minutes 'til golden brown.
7. Repeat with the remaining batter.
8. Serve the pancakes with fresh fruits, a drizzle of honey or maple syrup, if desired.

Per serving: Calories: 260kcal; Fat: 0.18oz; Carbs: 1.59oz; Protein: 0.32oz; Sodium: 210mg; Potassium: 0.0079oz; Phosphorus: 0.0081oz

5. Breakfast Tacos

Preparation time: 10 minutes

Cooking time: 15 minutes

Servings: 2

Ingredients:

- 1 tbsp extra-virgin olive oil
- 3/4 cups frozen bell peppers
- 1 tbsp water, divided
- 1/2 jalapeño pepper, minced
- 3 large eggs
- 1/8 tsp salt
- 1/8 tsp freshly ground black pepper
- 2 corn tortillas
- 1/4 cup shredded pepper jack cheese

Directions:

1. In your medium skillet, heat the olive oil over medium heat.

2. Add the bell peppers and stir. Add 1 tbsp of water then cover the pan—Cook for 3 to 4 minutes, or until the vegetables are thawed and hot.

3. Add the jalapeño pepper and cook for about 1 minute.

4. Then, combine the eggs and the remaining 1 tablespoon of water in your medium bowl and beat well.

5. Add the eggs to your skillet and cook for 4 to 6 minutes, occasionally stirring, until the eggs are set. Sprinkle with salt and pepper.

6. Heat your tortillas as directed on the package. Make the tacos with the tortillas, egg filling, and cheese, and serve.

Per serving: Calories: 283kcal; Fat: 0.67oz; Carbs: 0.53oz; Protein: 0.46oz; Sodium: 192mg; Potassium: 0.0078oz; Phosphorus: 0.0091oz

6. Baked Egg Custard

Preparation time: 15 minutes

Cooking time: 30 minutes

Servings: 4

Ingredients:

- 2 eggs, medium-sized
- 1/4 cup 2% milk
- 3 tbsp stevia
- 1 tsp lemon extract or vanilla
- 1 tsp nutmeg

Directions:

1. Preheat your oven to 325 deg.. Mix all the fixing, use an electric mixer to beat them for one minute until thoroughly mixed.

2. Pour the mixture into muffin pans or custard cups. Sprinkle a teaspoon nutmeg on top. Bake for approx. 30 minutes.

3. To confirm that the cake is ready, insert a knife in the center of the custard, which should come out clean

Per serving: Calories: 70kcal; Fat: 0oz; Carbs: 0.32oz; Protein: 0.11oz; Sodium: 34mg; Potassium: 0.0011oz; Phosphorus: 0.0015oz

7. Breakfast Wrap With Fruit And Cheese

Preparation time: 10 minutes

Cooking time: 0 minutes

Servings: 2

Ingredients:

- 2 tablespoons cream cheese
- 2 (6-inch) flour tortillas
- 1 tablespoon of honey
- 1 apple, sliced thin

Directions:

1. Spread 1 tbsp of cream cheese over each tortilla, leaving approximately 1/2 inch around the borders, and place both tortillas on a spotless work area.

1. On the tortilla's side that is closest to you, place the apple slices upon the cream cheese, leaving approximately 11/2 inches on either side and 2" on the bottom.

2. Lightly drizzle some honey over the apples.

3. Laying the edge of the tortilla over the apples, fold the right and left edges toward the center.

4. Fold the edge of the tortilla closest to you over the side pieces and the fruit. The tortilla should be rolled away from you to form a tight wrap.

5. The second tortilla should then be used.

Per serving: Calories: 188kcal; Fat: 0.21oz; Carbs: 1.16oz; Protein: 0.14oz; Sodium: 177mg; Potassium: 0.0048oz; Phosphorus: 0.0026oz

8. Cauliflower & Pear Porridge

Preparation time: 10 minutes

Cooking time: 25 minutes

Servings: 6

Ingredients:

- 2 cups pear, peeled, cored, and shredded
- ½ cup low-fat unsweetened coconut, shredded
- ½ cup cauliflower rice
- 1¾ cups fat-free milk
- 1 teaspoon organic vanilla extract
- ¾ cup fresh strawberries, hulled and sliced

Directions:

1. In a large-sized saucepan, stir together all ingredients except for strawberries over medium heat and bring it to a gentle boil.

2. Now, reduce the heat to low then simmer for approximately 15-20 minutes.

3. Serve warm with the topping of strawberries.

Per serving: Calories: 113kcal; Fat: 0.074oz; Carbs: 0.63oz; Protein: 0.18oz; Sodium: 64mg; Potassium: 0.0072oz; Phosphorus: 0.0102oz

9. Chicken Egg Breakfast Muffins

Preparation Time: 10 minutes

Cooking Time: 15 minutes

Servings: 2

Ingredients:

- 10 large eggs
- 1 cup of chicken breast, finely diced and cooked
- 3 tablespoons of scallions, finely chopped
- 1/4 teaspoon of onion powder
- Freshly ground black pepper and sea salt, according to taste

Directions:

1. Preheat your oven to 400 degrees Fahrenheit (204 degrees Celsius). Lightly grease a muffin pan with non-stick cooking spray and set aside.

2. In a sizable mixing bowl, beat the eggs thoroughly and season with onion powder, a pinch of salt, and black pepper. Fold in the diced chicken and scallions until evenly distributed.

3. Evenly distribute the egg mixture among the muffin cups, filling each about three-quarters full.

4. Place the muffin pan in the oven and bake for approximately 15 minutes, or until the muffins are set and lightly golden on top.

5. Remove from oven, let cool slightly, and serve warm.

Per serving: Calories: 71kcal; Fat: 0.14oz; Carbs: 0.014oz; Protein: 0.44oz; Sodium: 55mg; Potassium: 0.0045oz; Phosphorus: 0.0053oz

10. Yogurt Bulgur

Preparation time: 10 minutes

Cooking time: 15 minutes

Servings: 3

Ingredients:

- 1 cup bulgur
- 2 cups Greek yogurt
- 1 ½ cup water
- ½ teaspoon salt
- 1 teaspoon olive oil

Directions:

4. Pour olive oil in the saucepan and add bulgur.

5. Roast it over the medium heat for 2-3 minutes. Stir it from time to time.

6. After this, add salt and water.

7. Close the lid and cook bulgur for 15 minutes over the medium heat.

8. Then chill the cooked bulgur well and combine it with Greek yogurt. Stir it carefully.

9. Transfer the cooked meal into the serving plates. The yogurt bulgur tastes the best when it is cold.

Per serving: Calories: 274kcal; Fat: 0.17oz; Carbs: 1.44oz; Protein: 0.68oz; Sodium: 131mg; Potassium: 0.0084oz; Phosphorus: 0.0076oz

11. Easy Turnip Puree

Preparation Time: 10 minutes

Cooking Time: 12 minutes

Servings: 4

Ingredients:

- 1.5 pounds of turnips, peeled and diced
- 1 teaspoon of dill weed
- 3 slices of bacon, crisped and crumbled
- 2 tablespoons of chopped fresh chives

Instructions:

1. Place diced turnips in boiling water and let them cook for about 12 minutes. After cooking, thoroughly drain them and then transfer to a blender.

2. Incorporate the dill into the turnips and blend until the mixture achieves a smooth consistency.

3. Move the mashed turnips to a serving dish, garnishing them with the crumbled bacon and sprinkling chives over the top.

4. Ready to serve and enjoy.

Per Serving: Calories: 127kcal; Fat: 0.21oz; Carbs: 0.41oz; Protein: 0.24oz; Sodium: 86mg; Potassium: 0.0045oz; Phosphorus: 0.0039oz

12. Apple Omelet

Preparation time: 10 minutes

Cooking time: 8 minutes

Servings: 2

Ingredients:

- 6 egg whites
- ¼ cup fat-free milk
- 1 tablespoon water
- Freshly ground black pepper, as required
- 1 tablespoon olive oil
- 1 apple, peeled, cored, and thinly sliced
- ¾ cup onion, thinly sliced
- 2 tablespoons part-skim mozzarella cheese, shredded

Directions:

1. Preheat your oven to 400 deg. F.

2. In a glass bowl, add egg whites, milk, water, and black pepper and whisk well.

3. In a small-sized ovenproof wok, heat oil over medium heat and sauté apple and onion for approximately 5-6 minutes.

4. With the spatula, spread the apple mixture in the bottom of the wok.

5. Sprinkle with the cheese and top with the egg mixture evenly.

6. Transfer the wok to the oven and bake for approximately 10-12 minutes.

7. Remove the wok from the oven and cut the omelet into 2 equal-sized portions.

8. Serve warm.

Per serving: Calories: 218kcal; Fat: 0.31oz; Carbs: 0.77oz; Protein: 0.52oz; Sodium: 154mg; Potassium: 0.0094oz; Phosphorus: 0.0063oz

13. Breakfast Green Soup

Preparation time: 5 minutes

Cooking time: 5 minutes

Servings: 2

Ingredients:

- 2 cups chicken or vegetable broth, low sodium
- 1 halved avocado
- 1 cup of spinach
- 1 teaspoon of ground coriander
- 1 teaspoon of ground turmeric
- 1 teaspoon of ground cumin
- Freshly ground black pepper

Directions:

1. Add the avocado, spinach, broth, cumin, coriander, and turmeric to a blender until smooth, process.

2. Place the mixture in a small saucepan and heat for 2 to 3 minutes or until thoroughly cooked. Sprinkle with pepper.

Per serving: Calories: 221kcal; Fat: 0.63oz; Carbs: 0.53oz; Protein: 0.18oz; Sodium: 170mg; Potassium: 0.0089oz; Phosphorus: 0.0020oz

14. Italian Breakfast Frittata

Preparation time: 10 minutes

Cooking time: 45 minutes

Servings: 2

Ingredients:

- 1 cups egg whites
- 1/4 cup mozzarella cheese, shredded
- 1/2 cup cottage cheese, crumbled
- 1/8 cup fresh basil, sliced
- 1/4 cup roasted red peppers, sliced
- Salt & pepper to taste

Directions:

1. Preheat the oven to 375 deg. F.

2. Add all the ingredients into the large bowl and whisk well to combine.

3. Pour the frittata mixture into the baking dish and bake for 45 minutes. Slice and serve.

Per serving: Calories: 131kcal; Fat: 0.071oz; Carbs: 0.18oz; Protein: 0.78oz; Sodium: 75mg; Potassium: 0.0041oz; Phosphorus: 0.0039oz

15. Crunchy Granola Yogurt Bowl

Preparation time: 10 minutes

Cooking time: 0 minutes

Servings: 2

Ingredients:

- 2 cups plain whole-milk yogurt
- 3/4 tsp vanilla extract
- 1/2 cup granola
- 1/4 cup dried raisins
- 1/4 cup chopped pecans

Directions:

1. In your medium bowl, combine the yogurt and vanilla.

2. Layer the yogurt with granola, raisins, and pecans **into glasses or small bowls. Serve.**

Per serving: Calories: 360kcal; Fat: 0.60oz; Carbs: 1.55oz; Protein: 0.35oz; Sodium: 119mg; Potassium: 0.0098oz; Phosphorus: 0.0081oz

16. Pineapple Bread

Preparation time: 20 minutes

Cooking time: 1 hour

Servings: 10

Ingredients:

- 1/3 cup swerve
- 1/3 cup butter, unsalted
- 2 eggs
- 2 cups flour

- 3 teaspoons baking powder
- 1 cup pineapple, undrained
- 6 cherries, chopped

Directions:

1. Whisk the Swerve with the butter in a mixer until fluffy.

2. Stir in the eggs, then beat again.

3. Place the baking powder and flour, then mix well until smooth.

4. Fold in the cherries and pineapple.

5. Spread this cherry-pineapple batter in a 9x5 inch baking pan.

6. Bake the pineapple batter for 1 hour at 350 deg. F.

7. Slice the bread and serve.

Per serving: Calories: 197kcal; Fat: 0.25oz; Carbs: 0.14oz; Protein: 0.14oz; Sodium: 85mg; Potassium: 0.008oz; Phosphorus: 0.0083oz

17. Egg and Avocado Bake

Preparation time: 5 minutes

Cooking time: 15 minutes

Servings: 2

Ingredients:

- 2 large eggs
- 1 avocado, halved
- 1 tablespoon parsley, chopped
- Freshly ground black pepper

Directions:

1. The oven should be preheated at 425 deg. F.

2. Carefully crack one egg into a small basin while preserving the yolk.

3. The avocado halves should be placed cut-side up on a baking pan. Fill one half with the egg. Repeat with the remaining avocado and egg halves. Use pepper to season.

4. Bake the egg for 15 minutes or until it is set. After removing from the oven, top with fresh parsley. Serve.

Per serving: Calories: 242kcal; Fat: 0.71oz; Carbs: 0.32oz; Protein: 0.32oz; Sodium: 88mg; Potassium: 0.0097oz; Phosphorus: 0.0058oz

18. Celery and Kale Mix

Preparation time: 10 minutes

Cooking time: 20 minutes

Servings: 4

Ingredients:

- 2 celery stalks, chopped
- 5 cups kale, torn
- 1 small red bell pepper, chopped
- 3 tablespoons water
- 1 tablespoon coconut oil, melted

Directions:

1. Heat up a pan with the oil in a medium-high heat, add celery, stir and cook for 10 minutes.
2. Add kale, water, and bell pepper, stir and cook for 10 minutes more.
3. Divide between plates and serve.
4. Enjoy!

Per serving: Calories: 81kcal; Fat: 0.12oz; Carbs: 0.40oz; Protein: 0.10oz; Sodium: 75mg; Potassium: 0.0052oz; Phosphorus: 0.0042oz

19. Strawberry Muesli

Preparation time: 10 minutes

Cooking time: 30 minutes

Servings: 4

Ingredients:

- 2 cups Greek yogurt
- 1 ½ cup strawberries, sliced
- 1 ½ cup muesli
- 4 teaspoon maple syrup
- ¾ teaspoon ground cinnamon

Directions:

1. Put Greek yogurt in the food processor.
2. Add 1 cup of strawberries, maple syrup, and ground cinnamon.
3. Blend the ingredients until you get smooth mass.
4. Transfer the yogurt mass in the serving bowls.
5. Add Muesli and stir well.

6. Leave the meal for 30 minutes in the fridge.
7. After this, decorate it with remaining sliced strawberries.

Per serving: Calories: 149kcal; Fat: 2.6g; Carbs: 21.6g; Protein: 12g; Sodium: 151mg; Potassium: 227mg; Phosphorus: 216mg

20. Omelet with Feta and Fresh Mint

Preparation Time: 10 minutes

Cooking Time: 5 minutes

Servings: 1

Ingredients:

- 3 large eggs
- 1/4 cup of finely chopped fresh mint leaves
- 2 tablespoons of coconut milk
- 1/2 teaspoon of extra virgin olive oil
- 2 tablespoons of crumbled feta cheese
- A pinch of ground black pepper
- A dash of salt

Directions:

1. Combine the eggs, crumbled feta, chopped mint, coconut milk, a dash of pepper, and salt in a mixing bowl. Beat well to integrate.
2. Warm the extra virgin olive oil in a skillet over a gentle flame.
3. Once the pan is hot, add the beaten egg mixture and let it cook undisturbed until the bottom sets.
4. Carefully flip the omelet to cook the other side for an additional 2 minutes, ensuring it's cooked through yet tender.
5. Slide the omelet onto a plate, ready to be savored.

Per Serving: Calories: 275kcal; Fat: 0.71oz; Carbs: 0.14oz; Protein: 0.71oz; Sodium: 160mg; Potassium: 0.0095oz; Phosphorus: 0.0076oz

Chapter 2.   Smoothies, Juices, and Drinks

21. Hot Mulled Punch

Preparation time: 5 minutes

Cooking time: 10 minutes

Servings: 14

Ingredients:

- 4 sticks of cinnamon, broken
- ½ cup brown sugar
- 1 ½ teaspoons whole cloves
- 6 cups cranberry juice, unsweetened
- 8 cups apple juice, unsweetened

Directions:

1. Take a large pot, place it over medium-high heat, add all the ingredients in it, and stir until mixed.
2. Simmer the punch until hot and then serve.

Per serving: Calories: 135kcal; Fat: 0oz; Carbs: 1.16oz; Protein: 0oz; Sodium: 7mg; Potassium: 0.0094oz; Phosphorus: 0.0009oz

22. Mango and Pear Smoothie

Preparation time: 10 minutes

Cooking time: 0 minutes

Servings: 1

Ingredients:

- 1 ripe mango, cored and chopped
- ½ mango, peeled, pitted and chopped
- 1 cup kale, chopped
- ½ cup plain Greek yogurt
- 2 ice cubes

Directions:

1. Add pear, mango, yogurt, kale, and mango to a blender and puree
2. Add ice and blend until you have a smooth texture
3. Serve and enjoy!

Per serving: Calories: 293kcal; Fat: 0.28oz; Carbs: 1.87oz; Protein: 0.28oz; Sodium: 6mg; Potassium: 0.0028oz; Phosphorus: 0.0005oz

23. Mango Lassi Smoothie

Preparation time: 5 minutes

Cooking time: 0 minutes

Servings: 2

Ingredients:

- 1/2 cup plain yogurt
- 1/2 cup plain water
- 1/2 cup sliced mango
- 1 tbsp sugar
- 1/4 tsp cardamom
- 1/4 tsp cinnamon
- 1/4 cup lime juice

Directions:

1. Blend all the fixings in a blender until smooth.
2. Serve and enjoy!

Per serving: Calories: 89kcal; Fat: 0.071oz; Carbs: 0.50oz; Protein: 0.088oz; Sodium: 30mg; Potassium: 0.0065oz; Phosphorus: 0.0024oz

24. Strengthening Smoothie Bowl

Preparation time: 5 minutes

Cooking time: 4 minutes

Servings: 2

Ingredients:

- ¼ cup fresh blueberries
- ¼ cup fat-free plain Greek yogurt
- 1/3 cup unsweetened almond milk
- 2 tbsp. of whey protein powder
- 2 cups frozen blueberries

Directions:

1. In a blender, add blueberries and pulse for about 1 minute.
2. Add almond milk, yogurt and protein powder and pulse till desired consistency.
3. Transfer the mixture into 2 bowls evenly.
4. Serve with the topping of fresh blueberries.

Per serving: Calories: 176kcal; Fat: 0.074oz; Carbs:

0.95oz; Protein: 0.53oz; Sodium: 72mg; Potassium: 0.0085oz; Phosphorus: 0.009oz

25. Blueberry Shake

Preparation time: 5 minutes

Cooking time: 2 minutes

Servings: 4

Ingredients:

- 1 c. frozen blueberries
- 6 tbsp. protein powder
- 8 packets Splenda
- 14 oz. apple juice, unsweetened
- 8 cubes of ice

Directions:

1. Take a blender and place all the ingredients (in order) in it. Process for 1 minute until smooth.
2. Distribute the smoothie between four glasses and then serve.

Per serving: Calories: 162kcal; Fat: 0.018oz; Carbs: 1.06oz; Protein: 0.28oz; Sodium: 123.4mg; Potassium: 0.0079oz; Phosphorus: 0.0038oz

26. Pineapple Smoothie

Preparation time: 5 minutes

Cooking time: 0 minutes

Servings: 2

Ingredients:

- 1/4 cup crushed ice cubes
- 2 scoops of vanilla whey protein powder
- 1 cup water
- 1 1/2 cups pineapple

Directions:

1. Blend all the fixings in a blender until smooth.
2. Serve and enjoy!

Per serving: Calories: 117kcal; Fat: 0.071oz; Carbs: 0.64oz; Protein: 0.80oz; Sodium: 81mg; Potassium: 0.0104oz; Phosphorus: 0.0010oz

27. Honey Cinnamon Latte

Preparation time: 5 minutes

Cooking time: 5 minutes

Servings: 2

Ingredients:

- 1-½ cups of organic, unsweetened almond milk
- 1 scoop of organic vanilla protein powder
- 1 teaspoon of organic cinnamon
- ½ teaspoon of pure, local honey
- 1-2 shots of espresso

Directions:

1. Heat almond milk in the microwave 'til hot to the touch.
2. Add honey then stir until completely melted.
3. Using a whisk, add cinnamon, and protein powder and thoroughly combine.
4. Pour into a manual milk and froth concoction 'til foamy and creamy.
5. Pour espresso shots into a mug then add in milk mixture.

Per serving: Calories: 115kcal; Fat: 0.11oz; Carbs: 0.92oz; Protein: 0.11oz; Sodium: 125mg; Potassium: 0.0004oz; Phosphorus: 0.000004oz

28. Watermelon Kiwi Smoothie

Preparation time: 5 minutes

Cooking time: 0 minutes

Servings: 2

Ingredients:

- 2 cups watermelon chunks
- 1 kiwifruit, peeled
- 1 cup ice

Directions:

1. Blend all the fixings in a blender until smooth.
2. Serve and enjoy!

Per serving: Calories: 67kcal; Fat: 0g; Carbs: 17g; Protein: 1g; Sodium: 3mg; Potassium: 278mg; Phosphorus: 28mg

29. Almonds & Blueberries Smoothie

Preparation time: 5 minutes

Cooking time: 0 minutes

Servings: 2

Ingredients:

- 1/4 cup ground almonds, unsalted
- 1 cup fresh blueberries
- Fresh juice of 1 lemon

- 1 cup fresh kale leaf
- 1/2 cup coconut water
- 1 cup water
- 2 tbsp plain yogurt (optional)

Directions:

1. Blend all the fixings in a blender until smooth.
2. Serve and enjoy!

Per serving: Calories: 110kcal; Fat: 0.25oz; Carbs: 0.28oz; Protein: 0.071oz; Sodium: 101mg; Potassium: 0.0010oz; Phosphorus: 0.0006oz

30. Power-Boosting Smoothie

Preparation time: 5 minutes

Cooking time: 0 minutes

Servings: 2

Ingredients:

- ½ cup water
- ½ cup non-dairy whipped topping
- 2 scoops whey protein powder
- 1½ cups frozen blueberries

Directions:

1. In your high-speed blender, add all ingredients and pulse till smooth.
2. Transfer into 2 serving glass and serve immediately.

Per serving: Calories: 242kcal; Fat: 0.25oz; Carbs: 0.84oz; Protein: 0.82oz; Sodium: 63mg; Potassium: 0.0093oz; Phosphorus: 0.0011oz

31. Raspberry Peach Smoothie

Preparation time: 10minutes

Cooking time: 0 minutes

Servings: 2

Ingredients:

- 1 cup frozen raspberries
- 1 medium peach, pit removed, sliced
- ½ cup silken tofu
- 1 tbsp. honey
- 1 cup unsweetened vanilla almond milk

Directions:

1. First, start by putting all the ingredients in a blender jug.
2. Give it a pulse for 30 seconds until blended well.

3. Serve chilled and fresh.

Per serving: Calories: 132kcal; Fat: 0.21oz; Carbs: 0.49oz; Protein: 0.32oz; Sodium: 112mg; Potassium: 0.0092oz; Phosphorus: 0.0014oz

32. Minty Cherry Smoothie

Preparation time: 5 minutes

Cooking time: 0 minutes

Servings: 2

Ingredients:

- ¾ cup cherries
- 1 teaspoon mint
- ½ cup almond milk
- ½ cup kale
- ½ teaspoon fresh vanilla

Directions:

1. Wash and cut cherries
2. Take the pits out
3. Add cherries to the blender
4. Pour almond milk
5. Wash the mint and put two sprigs in blender
6. Separate the kale leaves from the stems
7. Put kale in a blender
8. Press vanilla bean and cut lengthwise with a knife
9. Scoop out your desired amount of vanilla and add to the blender
10. Blend until smooth
11. Serve chilled and enjoy!

Per serving: Calories: 200kcal; Fat: 0.35oz; Carbs: 0.49oz; Protein: 0.071oz; Sodium: 51mg; Potassium: 0.0055oz; Phosphorus: 0.0008oz

33. Blueberry Burst Smoothie

Preparation time: 5 minutes

Cooking time: 0 minutes

Servings: 2

Ingredients:

- 1 cup blueberries
- 1 cup chopped collard greens
- 1 cup unsweetened store-bought rice milk
- 1 tbsp almond butter
- 3 ice cubes

Directions:

1. Blend all the fixings in a blender until smooth.
2. Serve and enjoy!

Per serving: Calories: 131kcal; Fat: 0.21oz; Carbs: 0.67oz; Protein: 0.11oz; Sodium: 60mg; Potassium: 0.0051oz; Phosphorus: 0.0018oz

Per serving: Calories: 241kcal; Fat: 0.25oz; Carbs: 0.71oz; Protein: 0.92oz; Sodium: 420mg; Potassium: 0.0072oz; Phosphorus: 0.0004oz

34. Raspberry Peach Shake

Preparation time: 10minutes

Cooking time: 0 minutes

Servings: 2

Ingredients:

- 1 cup frozen raspberries
- 1 medium peach, pit removed, sliced
- ½ cup silken tofu
- 1 tbsp. honey
- 1 cup unsweetened vanilla almond milk

Directions:

1. First, start by putting all the ingredients in a blender jug.
2. Give it a pulse for 30 seconds until blended well.
3. Serve chilled and fresh.

Per serving: Calories: 132kcal; Fat: 0.11oz; Carbs: 0.49oz; Protein: 0.32oz; Sodium: 112mg; Potassium: 0.0092oz; Phosphorus: 0.0014oz

35. Pinna Colada Protein Shake

Preparation time: 5 minutes

Cooking time: 2 minutes

Servings: 1

Ingredients:

- 1/2 cup unsweetened vanilla almond milk
- 1/2 cup unsweetened coconut milk
- 3/4 cup frozen pineapple chunks
- 1 scoop vanilla protein powder
- 1 tsp raw honey
- 1 tsp vanilla

Directions:

1. Place almond milk, coconut milk, pineapple, vanilla protein powder, honey, and vanilla in a blender.
2. Blend until smooth. Serve immediately.

Chapter 3.   Appetizers

36. Cinnamon Apple Fries

Preparation time: 5 minutes

Cooking time: 15 minutes

Servings: 2

Ingredients:

- 2 apple, sliced thinly
- dash of cinnamon
- dash of stevia

Directions:

1. Coat the apple slices with cinnamon and stevia.
2. Bake them in your oven for 15 minutes at 325 deg. F until tender and crispy. Let it cool, and serve!

Per serving: Calories: 146kcal; Fat: 0.025oz; Carbs: 1.28oz; Protein: 0.056oz; Sodium: 10mg; Potassium: 0.0035oz; Phosphorus: 0oz

37. Carrot & Parsnips French Fries

Preparation time: 10 minutes

Cooking time: 20 minutes

Servings: 2

Ingredients:

- 6 large carrots, cut into thin sticks
- 6 large parsnips, cut into thin sticks
- 2 tbsp extra virgin olive oil
- 1/2 tsp sea salt

Directions:

1. Toss the carrots and parsnip sticks with extra virgin olive oil & salt in a bowl. Spread them into a baking sheet covered with parchment paper.
2. Bake the sticks in your oven at 425 deg. F for 20 minutes or until browned. Serve!

Per serving: Calories: 179kcal; Fat: 0.14oz; Carbs: 0.49oz; Protein: 0.39oz; Sodium: 27.3mg; Potassium: 0.0079oz; Phosphorus: 0.0041oz

38. Marinated Berries

Preparation time: 5 minutes

Cooking time: 30 minutes

Servings: 2

Ingredients:

- 1 cups fresh strawberries, hulled and quartered
- 1/2 cup fresh blueberries (optional)
- 1 tablespoons sugar
- 1/2 tablespoon balsamic vinegar
- 1 tablespoons chopped fresh mint (optional)
- 1/8 teaspoon freshly ground black pepper

Directions:

1. Gently toss the strawberries, blueberries (if using), sugar, vinegar, mint (if using), and pepper in a large nonreactive bowl.
2. Let the flavors blend for at least 25 minutes or as long as 2 hours.

Per serving: Calories: 73kcal; Fat: 0.28oz; Carbs: 0.63oz; Protein: 0.035oz; Sodium: 4mg; Potassium: 0.0057oz; Phosphorus: 0.0047oz

39. Mango Cucumber Salsa

Preparation time: 10 minutes + chilling time

Cooking time: 0 minutes

Servings: 2

Ingredients:

- 1 cup cucumber, chopped
- 2 cups mango, diced
- 1/2 cup cilantro, minced
- 2 tbsp fresh lime juice
- 1 tbsp scallions, minced
- 1/4 tsp chipotle powder
- 1/4 tsp sea salt

Directions:

1. Mix the ingredients in a bowl then refrigerate until ready to serve.

Per serving: Calories: 155kcal; Fat: 0.021oz; Carbs:

1.35oz; Protein: 0.049oz; Sodium: 3.2mg; Potassium: 0.0078oz; Phosphorus: 0.0010oz

40. Popcorn With Sugar And Spice

Preparation time: 10 minutes

Cooking time: 10 minutes

Servings: 2

Ingredients:

- 8 cups hot popcorn
- 2 tablespoons unsalted butter
- 2 tablespoons sugar
- 1/2 teaspoon cinnamon
- 1/4 teaspoon nutmeg

Directions:

1. Popping the corn, put aside.
2. Heat the butter, sugar, cinnamon, and nutmeg in the microwave or saucepan over a range fire 'til the butter is melted, and the sugar dissolves.
3. Sprinkle the corn with the spicy butter, and mix well.
4. Serve immediately for optimal flavor.

Per serving: Calories: 120kcal; Fat: 0.25oz; Carbs: 0.42oz; Protein: 0.071oz; Sodium: 2mg; Potassium: 0.0020oz; Phosphorus: 0.0021oz

41. Vegetable Rolls

Preparation time: 30 minutes

Cooking time: 0 minutes

Servings: 8

Ingredients:

- ½ cup finely shredded red cabbage
- ½ cup grated carrot
- ¼ cup julienne red bell pepper
- ¼ cup, julienned scallion both green and white parts
- ¼ cup chopped cilantro
- 1 tablespoon olive oil
- ¼ teaspoon ground cumin
- ¼ teaspoon freshly ground black pepper
- 1 English cucumber sliced very thin strips

Directions:

1. In a bowl, toss together the black pepper, cumin, olive oil, cilantro, scallion, red pepper, carrot, and cabbage. Mix well.
2. Evenly divide the vegetable filling among the cucumber strips, placing the filling close to one end of the strip.
3. Roll up the cucumber strips around the filling and secure with a wooden pick.
4. Repeat with each cucumber strip.

Per serving: Calories: 26kcal; Fat: 0.071oz; Carbs: 0.11oz; Protein: 0oz; Sodium: 7mg; Potassium: 0.0002oz; Phosphorus: 0.0005oz

42. Egg and Veggie Fajitas

Preparation time: 15 minutes

Cooking time: 10 minutes

Servings: 4

Ingredients:

- 3 large eggs
- 3 egg whites
- 2 teaspoons chili powder
- 1 tablespoon unsalted butter
- 1 onion, chopped
- 2 garlic cloves, minced
- 1 jalapeño pepper, minced
- 1 red bell pepper, chopped
- 1 cup frozen corn, thawed and drained
- 8 (6-inch) corn tortillas

Directions:

1. Whisk the eggs, egg whites, and chili powder in a small bowl until well combined. Set aside.
2. Prepare a huge skillet and melt the butter on medium heat.
3. Sauté the onion, garlic, jalapeño, bell pepper, and corn until the vegetables are tender, 3 to 4 minutes.
4. Place the beaten egg mixture to the skillet. Cook, occasionally stirring, until the eggs form large curds and are set, 3 to 5 minutes.
5. Meanwhile, soften the corn tortillas as directed on the package.
6. Divide the egg mixture evenly among the softened corn tortillas. Roll the tortillas up and serve.

Per serving: Calories: 316kcal; Fat: 0.49oz; Carbs:

Directions:

1.23oz; Protein: 0.49oz; Sodium: 167mg; Potassium: 0.0073oz; Phosphorus: 0.0066oz

43. Vinegar & Salt Kale

Preparation time: 10 minutes

Cooking time: 12 minutes

Servings: 2

Ingredients:

- 1 head kale, chopped
- 1 tsp extra virgin olive oil
- 1 tbsp apple cider vinegar
- 1/2 tsp sea salt

Directions:

1. Mix the kale, vinegar, and olive oil in a bowl. Sprinkle with salt and massage the ingredients with your hands.
2. Spread the kale onto 2 paper-lined baking sheets and bake in your oven at 375 deg. F for 12 minutes or until crispy. Let it cool within 10 minutes before serving.

Per serving: Calories: 152kcal; Fat: 0.29oz; Carbs: 0.54oz; Protein: 0.14oz; Sodium: 120mg; Potassium: 0.0072oz; Phosphorus: 0.0013oz

44. Lemon Chicken & Avocado Salad

Preparation time: 20 minutes

Cooking time: 10 minutes Servings: 4

Ingredients:

- 2 cooked and chopped chicken breasts
- 1 ripe avocado, cubed
- 1/4 red onion, finely chopped
- 2 tablespoons of fresh lemon juice
- 2 tablespoons extra virgin olive oil
- 1/4 teaspoon ground black pepper

Fresh herbs to taste (basil, parsley, cilantro), chopped

Lettuce or baby spinach for serving

Directions:

1. In a large bowl, combine the chopped chicken, cubed avocado, and red onion.
2. In a small bowl, mix the lemon juice, olive oil, and black pepper.
3. Pour the dressing over the chicken and gently mix to combine.
4. Add the chopped fresh herbs and mix again.
5. Serve on a bed of lettuce or baby spinach.

Per serving: Calories: 230kcal; Fat: 0.53oz; Carbohydrates: 0.21oz; Protein: 0.71oz; Sodium: 70mg; Potassium: 0.0159oz; Phosphorus: 0.0053oz

45. Spicy Crab Dip

Preparation time: 10 minutes

Cooking time: 20 minutes

Servings: 2

Ingredients:

- 2 can of 8 oz. softened cream cheese
- 2 tbsp. finely chopped onions
- 2 tbsp. lemon juice
- 4 tbsp. Worcestershire sauce
- 1/4 tsp. black pepper cayenne pepper to taste
- 4 tbsp. to s. of almond milk or non-fortified rice drink
- 2 can of 6 oz. of crabmeat

Directions:

1. Preheat the oven to 375 deg. F.
2. Pour the cheese cream into a bowl. Add the onions, lemon juice, Worcestershire sauce, black pepper, and cayenne pepper. Mix well. Stir in the almond milk/rice drink.
3. Add the crabmeat and mix until you obtain a homogeneous mixture.
4. Pour the mixture into a baking dish. Cook without covering for 15 minutes or until bubbles appear. Serve hot with triangle-cut pita bread.
5. Microwave until bubbles appear, about 4 minutes, stirring every 1 to 2 minutes.

Per serving: Calories: 42kcal; Fat: 0.035oz; Carbs: 0.071oz; Protein: 0.25oz; Sodium: 167mg; Potassium: 0.0046oz; Phosphorus: 0.0049oz

46. Easy Egg Salad

Preparation time: 5 minutes

Cooking time: 8 minutes

Servings: 4

Ingredients:

- ¼ cup of celery, chopped
- 1 tbsp. of yellow mustard

- 1 tsp of smoked paprika
- 3 tbsp. of mayo

Directions:

1. Hard boil the eggs in a small pot filled with water for approx. 7-8 minutes. Leave the eggs in the water for an extra couple of minutes before peeling.
2. Peel the eggs then chop finely with a knife or tool.
3. Combine all the chopped veggies with the mayo and mustard. Add in the eggs and mix well.
4. Sprinkle with some smoked paprika on top.
5. Serve cold with pitta, white bread slices, or lettuce wraps.

Per serving: Calories: 127kcal; Fat: 0.46oz; Carbs: 0.21oz; Protein: 0.25oz; Sodium: 170.7mg; Potassium: 0.0031oz; Phosphorus: 0.0036oz

47. Braised Cabbage

Preparation time: 10 minutes

Cooking time: 10 minutes

Servings: 4

Ingredients:

- 1 small cabbage head, shredded
- 2 tablespoons water
- A drizzle of olive oil
- 6 ounces shallots, cooked and chopped
- A pinch of black pepper
- A pinch of sweet paprika
- 1 tablespoon dill, chopped

Directions:

6. Heat up a pan with the oil over medium heat, add the cabbage and the water, stir and sauté for 5 minutes.
7. Place the rest of the ingredients, toss, cook for 5 minutes more, divide everything between plates and serve as a side dish!
8. Enjoy!

Per serving: Calories: 91kcal; Fat: 0.018oz; Carbs: 0.73oz; Protein: 0.14oz; Sodium: 75mg; Potassium: 0.0045oz; Phosphorus: 0.0042oz

48. Buffalo Chicken Dip

Preparation time: 10 minutes

Cooking time: 3 hours

Servings: 2

Ingredients:

- 2-ounce cream cheese
- 1/4 cup bottled roasted red peppers
- 1/2 cup reduced-fat sour cream
- 2 teaspoons hot pepper sauce
- 1 cup cooked, shredded chicken

Directions:

1. Blend half a cup of drained red peppers in a food processor until smooth.
2. Now, thoroughly mix cream cheese and sour cream with the pureed peppers in a bowl.
3. Stir in shredded chicken and hot sauce, then transfer the mixture to a slow cooker.
4. Cook for 3 hours on low heat.
5. Serve warm with celery, carrots, cauliflower, and cucumber.

Per serving: Calories: 73kcal; Fat: 0.18oz; Carbs: 0.071oz; Protein: 0.18oz; Sodium: 66mg; Potassium: 0.0029oz; Phosphorus: 0.0017oz

49. Herbed Cream Cheese Tartines

Preparation time: 10 minutes

Cooking time: 15 minutes

Servings: 2

Ingredients:

- 1 clove garlic, halved
- 1 cup cream cheese spread
- 1/4 cup chopped herbs
- 2 tbsp minced French shallot or onion
- 1/2 tsp black pepper
- 2 tbsp water

Directions:

1. Combine the cream cheese, herbs, shallot, pepper, and water in a medium-sized bowl with a hand blender.
2. Serve the cream cheese with the rusks.

Per serving: Calories: 476kcal; Fat: 0.32oz; Carbs: 2.65oz; Protein: 0.81oz; Sodium: 185mg; Potassium: 0.011oz; Phosphorus: 0.0040oz

50. Roasted Mint Carrots

Preparation time: 20 minutes

Cooking time: 5 minutes

Servings: 6

Ingredients:

- 1 pound carrots, trimmed
- 1 tablespoon extra-virgin olive oil
- freshly ground black pepper
- ¼ cup thinly sliced mint

Directions:

1. Preheat the oven to 425 deg. F.
2. Assemble the carrots in a single layer on a rimmed baking sheet. Drizzle with the olive oil, and shake the carrots on the sheet to coat. Season with pepper.
3. Cook for 20 minutes, or until tender and browned, stirring twice while cooking. Sprinkle with the mint and serve.
4. Substitution tip: To lower the potassium in this dish, use 8 ounces of carrots and 8 ounces of turnips cut into cubes. This will cut the potassium to 193mg.

Per serving: Calories: 51kcal; Fat: 0.071oz; Carbs: 0.25oz; Protein: 0.035oz; Sodium: 52mg; Potassium: 0.0085oz; Phosphorus: 0.0009oz

Chapter 4.   First Courses

51. Cod & Green Bean Risotto

Preparation time: 4 minutes

Cooking time: 40 minutes

Servings: 2

Ingredients:

- ½ cup arugula
- 1 finely diced white onion
- 4 oz. cod fillet
- 1 cup white rice
- 2 lemon wedges
- 1 cup boiling water
- ¼ tsp. black pepper
- 1 cup low-sodium chicken broth
- 1 tbsp. extra virgin olive oil
- ½ cup green beans

Directions:

1. Warm-up oil in a large pan on medium heat. Sauté the chopped onion for 5 minutes until soft before adding in the rice and stirring for 1-2 minutes.
2. Combine the broth with boiling water. Add half of the liquid to the pan and stir. Slowly add the remaining liquid while stirring for up to 20-30 minutes.
3. Stir in the green beans to the risotto. Place the fish on top of the rice, cover, and steam for 10 minutes.
4. Use your fork to break up the fish fillets and stir them into the rice. Sprinkle with freshly ground pepper to serve and a squeeze of fresh lemon. Serve with lemon wedges and arugula.

Per serving: Calories: 221kcal; Fat: 0.28oz; Carbs: 1.02oz; Protein: 0.42oz; Sodium: 198mg; Potassium: 0.0087oz; Phosphorus: 0.0050oz

52. Roasted Peach Open-Face Sandwich

Preparation time: 5 minutes

Cooking time: 15 minutes

Servings: 2

Ingredients:

- 1 fresh peaches, peeled & sliced
- 1/2 tbsp extra-virgin olive oil
- 1/2 tbsp freshly squeezed lemon juice
- 1/8 tsp salt
- 1/8 tsp freshly ground black pepper
- 2 oz cream cheese, at room temperature
- 1 tsp fresh thyme leaves
- 2 bread slices

Directions:

1. Preheat the oven to 400 deg. F.
2. Arrange the peaches on a rimmed baking sheet. Brush them with olive oil on both sides.
3. Roast the peaches for 10–15 minutes until they are lightly golden brown around the edges. Sprinkle with lemon juice, salt, and pepper.
4. Combine the cream cheese plus thyme in a small bowl and mix well.
5. Toast your bread, then spread it with the cream cheese mixture. Top with the peaches and serve.

Per serving: Calories: 250kcal; Fat: 0.46oz; Carbs: 0.99oz; Protein: 0.21oz; Sodium: 176mg; Potassium: 0.0092oz; Phosphorus: 0.0057oz

53. Ground Turkey With Veggies

Preparation time: 15 minutes

Cooking time: 12 minutes

Servings: 2

Ingredients:

- 1/2 tablespoon sesame oil
- 1/2 tablespoon coconut oil
- 1/2-pound lean ground turkey
- 1 tablespoons fresh ginger, minced
- 1 minced garlic cloves
- 1/2 (16-ounce) bag of the vegetable mix (broccoli, carrot, cabbage, kale, and brussels sprouts)
- ¼ cup coconut aminos
- 1 tablespoons balsamic vinegar

Directions:

1. In a big skillet, heat both oils on medium-high

heat. Add turkey, ginger, and garlic and cook for approximately 5-6 minutes.

2. Add vegetable mix and cook for about 4-5 minutes. Stir in coconut aminos and vinegar and cook for about 1 minute. Serve hot.

Per serving: Calories: 234kcal; Fat: 0.32oz; Carbs: 0.32oz; Protein: 1.02oz; Sodium: 115mg; Potassium: 0.0032oz; Phosphorus: 0.0005oz

54. Eggplant Casserole

Preparation time: 10 minutes

Cooking time: 25-30 minutes

Servings: 2

Ingredients:

- 3 cups eggplant, peeled & cut into large chunks
- 2 egg whites
- 1 large egg, whole
- 1/2 cup non-dairy vegetable cream
- 1/4 tsp sage
- 1/2 cup breadcrumbs
- 1 tbsp margarine, melted
- 1/4 tsp garlic salt
- Pepper to taste

Directions:

1. Warm the oven to 350 deg. F.
2. Place the eggplant chunks in a medium pan, cover with a bit of water and cook with the lid covered until tender. Drain from the water and mash with a tool or fork.
3. Beat the eggs with non-dairy vegetable cream, sage, salt, and pepper. Whisk in the eggplant mush. Combine the melted margarine with the breadcrumbs.
4. Bake in the oven within 20-25 minutes or until the casserole has a golden-brown crust.

Per serving: Calories: 186kcal; Fat: 0.32oz; Carbs: 0.67oz; Protein: 0.25oz; Sodium: 203mg; Potassium: 0.0046oz; Phosphorus: 0.0022oz

55. Ginger Shrimp With Snow Peas

Preparation time: 20 minutes

Cooking time: 12 minutes

Servings: 2

Ingredients:

- 1 tbsp extra-virgin olive oil
- 1/2 tbsp minced peeled fresh ginger
- 1 cups snow peas
- 3/4 cups frozen baby peas
- 1 1/2 tbsp water
- 1/2-pound medium shrimp, shelled & deveined
- 1 tbsp low-sodium soy sauce
- 1/8 tsp freshly ground black pepper

Directions:

1. In your large skillet, heat the olive oil over medium heat. Add the ginger and stir-fry for 1 to 2 minutes until the ginger is fragrant.
2. Add the snow peas and stir-fry within 2 to 3 minutes until they are tender-crisp.
3. Add the baby peas and the water and stir. Cover the wok and steam for 2 to 3 minutes or until the vegetables are tender.
4. Stir in the shrimp and stir-fry for 3 to 4 minutes, or until the shrimp have curled and turned pink. Add the soy sauce and pepper; stir and serve.

Per serving: Calories: 237kcal; Fat: 0.25oz; Carbs: 0.42oz; Protein: 1.13oz; Sodium: 169mg; Potassium: 0.0072oz; Phosphorus: 0.0088oz

56. Vegetable Stew

Preparation time: 15 minutes

Cooking time: 15 minutes

Servings: 8

Ingredients:

- 1 teaspoon olive oil
- 1 sweet onion, chopped
- 1 teaspoon minced garlic
- 2 zucchinis, chopped
- 1 red bell pepper, diced
- 2 carrots, chopped
- 2 cups low-sodium vegetable stock
- 2 cups broccoli florets
- 1 teaspoon ground coriander
- ½ teaspoon ground cumin
- Pinch cayenne pepper
- Freshly ground black pepper
- 2 tablespoons chopped fresh cilantro

Directions:

1. Cook garlic & onion in a saucepan until softened.

2. Put zucchini, bell pepper, and carrots, and sauté for 5 minutes.
3. Mix vegetable stock, broccoli, coriander, cumin, and cayenne pepper.
4. Let it boil and simmer to medium-low until the vegetables are tender, often stirring about 5 minutes.
5. Add pepper and serve hot, topped with the cilantro.

Per serving: Calories: 45kcal; Fat: 0.035oz; Carbs: 0.18oz; Protein: 0.035oz; Sodium: 194mg; Potassium: 0.0065oz; Phosphorus: 0.0007oz

57. Turkey Broccoli Salad

Preparation time: 10 minutes

Cooking time: 0 minutes

Servings: 2

Ingredients:

- 4 cups broccoli florets
- 1 1/2 cooked chicken breast halves, skinless, boneless, cubed
- 3 green onions, chopped
- 1/2 cup mayonnaise
- 1/8 cup apple cider vinegar
- 1/8 cup honey

Directions:

1. Combine the broccoli, chicken, and green onions in a large bowl.
2. Whisk the mayonnaise, vinegar, and honey in a bowl until well blended.
3. Pour the mayonnaise dressing over your broccoli mixture, and toss to coat. Cover and refrigerate until chilled, if desired. Serve

Per serving: Calories: 125kcal; Fat: 0.25oz; Carbs: 0.46oz; Protein: 0.18oz; Sodium: 23mg; Potassium: 0.0055oz; Phosphorus: 0.0052oz

58. White Fish Stew

Preparation time: 10 minutes

Cooking time: 15-20 minutes

Servings: 2

Ingredients:

- 4 white fish fillets
- 1 cup water

- 1 onion, sliced
- 1/2 tsp paprika
- 1/4 cup olive oil
- 1/4 tsp pepper
- 1/4 tsp salt

Directions:

1. Add the olive oil, paprika, onion, water, pepper, and salt into the saucepan. Stir well and let it boil over medium-high heat.
2. Adjust to medium-low heat and simmer for 15 minutes. Add the white fish fillets and simmer until the fish is cooked. Serve and enjoy.

Per serving: Calories: 513kcal; Fat: 1.14oz; Carbs: 0.13oz; Protein: 1.79oz; Sodium: 75mg; Potassium: 0.0041oz; Phosphorus: 0.0042oz

59. Shrimp Quesadilla

Preparation time: 10 minutes + marinating time

Cooking time: 17-18 minutes

Servings: 2

Ingredients:

- 5 oz shrimp, shelled & deveined
- 4 tbsp Mexican salsa
- 2 tbsp fresh cilantro, chopped
- 1 tbsp lemon juice
- 1 tsp ground cumin
- 1 tsp cayenne pepper
- 2 tbsp unsweetened soy yogurt or creamy tofu
- 2 medium corn flour tortillas
- 2 tbsp low-fat cheddar cheese

Directions:

1. Mix the cilantro, cumin, lemon juice, and cayenne in a Ziploc bag. Add the shrimps and marinate within 10 minutes.
2. Heat a pan in a medium heat with some olive oil and toss the shrimp with the marinade.
3. Let cook for a couple of minutes or as soon as shrimps have turned pink and opaque.
4. Add the soy cream or soft tofu to the pan and mix well. Remove from the heat and keep the marinade aside.
5. Heat tortillas in the grill or microwave for a few seconds.
6. Place 2 tbsp salsa on each tortilla. Top one tortilla

with the shrimp mixture, add the cheese on top and stack one tortilla against each other.

7. Transfer this to a baking tray and cook for 7–8 minutes at 350 deg. F to melt the cheese and crisp the tortillas. Serve warm

Per serving: Calories: 255kcal; Fat: 0.32oz; Carbs: 0.74oz; Protein: 0.85oz; Sodium: 162mg; Potassium: 0.0048oz; Phosphorus: 0.0031oz

60. Traditional Black Bean Chili

Preparation time: 10 minutes

Cooking time: 4 hours

Servings: 2

Ingredients:

- 3/4 cups red bell pepper, chopped
- 1/2 cup yellow onion, chopped
- 3/4 cups mushrooms, sliced
- 1/2 tablespoon olive oil
- 1/2 tablespoon chili powder
- 1 garlic cloves, minced
- 1/2 teaspoon chipotle chili pepper, chopped
- 1/4 teaspoon cumin, ground
- 8 ounces canned black beans, drained & rinsed
- 1 tablespoons cilantro, chopped
- 1/2 cup red bell peppers, chopped

Directions:

1. Add red bell peppers, onion, dill, mushrooms, chili powder, garlic, chili pepper, cumin, black beans, and Red bell peppers to your Slow Cooker.
2. Stir well.
3. Place lid and cook on HIGH for 4 hours.
4. Sprinkle cilantro on top.
5. Serve and enjoy!

Per serving: Calories: 211kcal; Fat: 0.11oz; Carbs: 0.78oz; Protein: 0.18oz; Sodium: 75mg; Potassium: 0.0038oz; Phosphorus: 0.0032oz

61. Grilled Chicken Pizza

Preparation time: 20 minutes

Cooking time: 15 minutes

Servings: 2

Ingredients:

- 2 pita bread
- 3 tbsp. low sodium BBQ sauce
- 1/4 bowl red onion
- 4 oz. cooked chicken
- 2 tbsp. crumbled feta cheese
- 1/8 tsp. garlic powder

Directions:

1. Preheat oven to 350 deg. F.
2. Place two pitas on the pan after you have put non-stick cooking spray on it.
3. Spread BBQ sauce (2 tablespoons) on the pita.
4. Cut the onion and put it on the pita. Cube chicken and put it on the pitas.
5. Put both feta and garlic powder over the pita.
6. Bake for 12 minutes. Serve and enjoy!

Per serving: Calories: 320kcal; Fat: 0.21oz; Carbs: 0.92oz; Protein: 0.78oz; Sodium: 220mg; Potassium: 0.0053oz; Phosphorus: 0.0042oz

62. Spinach And Crab Soup

Preparation time: 15 minutes

Cooking time: 10 minutes

Servings: 2

Ingredients:

- 1 tbsp extra-virgin olive oil
- 1 shallots, minced
- 4 oz fresh lump crab meat, picked over
- 2 cups low-sodium vegetable broth
- 1 cups roughly chopped baby spinach leaves
- 1/4 tsp old bay seasoning
- 1/8 tsp freshly ground black pepper

Directions:

1. In your medium saucepan, heat the olive oil over medium heat—Cook the shallots for about 3 minutes, stirring, until tender.
2. Add the crab meat and cook for 1 minute. Place the vegetable broth then bring to a simmer. Reduce the heat to low.
3. Add the spinach leaves, Old Bay Seasoning mix, and pepper. Simmer until your spinach is wilted and the soup is hot. Serve.

Per serving: Calories: 138kcal; Fat: 0.25oz; Carbs: 0.21oz; Protein: 0.42oz; Sodium: 208mg; Potassium: 0.0051oz; Phosphorus: 0.0056oz

63. Chicken & Veggie Casserole

Preparation time: 15 minutes

Cooking time: 30 minutes

Servings: 2

Ingredients:

- 1/3 cup Dijon mustard
- 1/3 cup organic honey
- 1 teaspoon dried basil
- ¼ teaspoon ground turmeric
- 1 teaspoon dried basil, crushed
- Salt
- Ground black pepper
- 1¾ pound chicken breasts
- 1 cup fresh white mushrooms, sliced
- ½ head broccoli, cut into small florets

Directions:

1. Warm oven to 350 deg. F. Lightly greases a baking dish. Mix all ingredients except chicken, mushrooms, and broccoli in a bowl.
2. Put the chicken in your prepared baking dish, then top with mushroom slices. Place broccoli florets around the chicken evenly.
3. Pour 1 / 2 of the honey mixture over the chicken and broccoli. Bake for approximately 20 minutes. Now, coat the chicken with the remaining sauce and bake for about 10 minutes.

Per serving: Calories: Calories: 427kcal; Fat: 0.32oz; Carbs: 0.56oz; Protein: 1.23oz; Sodium: 1mg; Potassium: 0.0081oz; Phosphorus: 0.0054oz

64. Creamy Mushroom Pasta

Preparation time: 10 minutes

Cooking time: 20 minutes

Servings: 2

Ingredients:

- 12 oz whole-grain fettuccine pasta
- 3 tbsp extra-virgin olive oil
- 1 (8-oz) package of button mushrooms, sliced
- 3 garlic cloves, sliced
- 1 cup heavy cream
- Pinch of salt
- Freshly ground black pepper to taste

Directions:

1. Boil a large pot of water. Add the pasta and cook within 9 to 10 minutes, until al dente. Drain, reserving 1/3 cup of the pasta water, and set aside.
2. Meanwhile, heat the olive oil on medium-high heat in your large, heavy saucepan. Add the mushrooms in a single layer.
3. Cook within 3 minutes or until the mushrooms are golden brown on one side. Carefully turn the mushrooms and cook for another 2 minutes.
4. Adjust to medium heat and add the garlic. Sauté, stirring, for 2 minutes longer, until the garlic is fragrant.
5. Add the cream to your skillet with the mushrooms and season with salt and pepper. Simmer for 3 minutes or until the mixture starts to thicken.
6. Add the drained pasta to your pan and coat using tongs. Add the reserved pasta water, if necessary, to loosen the sauce. Serve.

Per serving: Calories: 405kcal; Fat: 0.81oz; Carbs: 1.55oz; Protein: 0.35oz; Sodium: 42mg; Potassium: 0.0074oz; Phosphorus: 0.0054oz

65. Vegetable Fried Rice

Preparation time: 20 minutes

Cooking time: 20 minutes

Servings: 6

Ingredients:

- 1 tablespoon olive oil
- ½, chopped sweet onion
- 1 tablespoon grated fresh ginger
- 2 teaspoons minced garlic
- 1 cup sliced carrots
- ½ cup chopped eggplant
- ½ cup peas
- ½ cup green beans cut into 1-inch pieces
- 2 tablespoon chopped fresh cilantro
- 3 cups cooked rice

Directions:

1. Heat the olive oil in a skillet.
2. Sauté the ginger, onion, and garlic for 3 minutes or until softened.
3. Stir in carrot, eggplant, green beans, and peas and sauté for 3 minutes more.
4. Add cilantro and rice.

5. Sauté, continually stirring, for about 10 minutes or until the rice is heated through.
6. Serve.

Per serving: Calories: 189kcal; Fat: 0.25oz; Carbs: 0.99oz; Protein: 0.21oz; Sodium: 13mg; Potassium: 0.0061oz; Phosphorus: 0.0031oz

66. Grilled Chicken With Pineapple & Veggies

Preparation time: 20 or so minutes
Cooking time: 22 minutes
Servings: 2
Ingredients:

For Sauce:

- 1/2 garlic clove, minced.
- 1/2 teaspoon fresh ginger, minced
- 1/4 cup coconut aminos
- 1/8 cup fresh pineapple juice
- 1 tablespoons freshly squeezed lemon juice
- 1 tablespoons balsamic vinegar
- 1/8 teaspoon red pepper flakes, crushed
- Salt
- Ground black pepper

For Grilling:

- 2 skinless, boneless chicken breasts
- 1/2 pineapple, peeled and sliced
- 1/2 bell pepper, seeded and cubed
- 1/2 zucchini, sliced
- 1/2 red onion, sliced

Directions:

1. For sauce in a pan, mix all ingredients on medium-high heat. Bring to a boil reducing the heat to medium-low. Cook for approximately 5-6 minutes.
2. Remove, then keep aside to cool down slightly. Coat the chicken breasts about ¼ from the sauce. Keep aside for approximately half an hour.
3. Preheat the grill to medium-high heat. Grease the grill grate. Grill the chicken pieces for around 5-8 minutes per side.
4. Now, squeeze pineapple and vegetables on the grill grate. Grill the pineapple within 3 minutes per side. Grill the vegetables for approximately 4-5 minutes, stirring once inside the middle way.
5. Cut the chicken breasts into desired-size slices, and divide the chicken, pineapple, and vegetables

into serving plates. Serve alongside the remaining sauce.

Per serving: Calories: 435kcal; Fat: 0.42oz; Carbs: 0.88oz; Protein: 1.34oz; Sodium: 155mg; Potassium: 0.0047oz; Phosphorus: 0.0030oz

67. Pad Thai

Preparation time: 15 minutes
Cooking time: 20 minutes
Servings: 2
Ingredients:

- 4 oz whole-grain spaghetti or capellini
- 1 1/2 tbsp extra-virgin olive oil
- 1 cups frozen stir-fry vegetables
- 1/4 cup peanut butter
- 1 tbsp low-sodium soy sauce
- 1/8 tsp freshly ground black pepper
- 1/2 lime, juiced and zested

Directions:

1. Boil a large pot of water. Add your pasta, then boil until al dente. Remove ⅓ cup of the pasta water and set it aside. Drain the pasta and also set it aside.
2. In your large saucepan, heat the olive oil over medium-high heat. Place the vegetables, reduce the heat to medium, and stir-fry for 3 to 6 minutes, or until they are thawed.
3. Meanwhile, in your small bowl, combine the peanut butter, reserved pasta water, soy sauce, and pepper and beat well.
4. Add the drained pasta and stir-fry for 2 minutes or until hot when the vegetables are thawed.
5. Add the peanut butter sauce. Stir-fry until your sauce has thickened and coats the pasta. Stir in the lime juice & zest, and serve.

Per serving: Calories: 453kcal; Fat: 0.78oz; Carbs: 1.98oz; Protein: 0.53oz; Sodium: 197mg; Potassium: 0.0077oz; Phosphorus: 0.0059oz

68. Sautéed Green Beans

Preparation time: 10 minutes
Cooking time: 15 minutes
Servings: 2
Ingredients:

- 1 cups frozen green beans
- 1/4 cup red bell pepper
- 2 tsps. margarine
- 1/8 cup onion
- 1/2 tsp dried dill weed
- 1/2 tsp dried parsley
- 1/8 tsp black pepper

Directions:

1. Cook green beans in a huge pan of boiling water until tender, then drain.
2. While cooking beans, melt the margarine in a skillet and fry the other vegetables.
3. Add the beans to sautéed vegetables.
4. Sprinkle with freshly ground pepper then serve with meat and fish dishes.

Per serving: Calories: 67kcal; Fat: 0.28oz; Carbs: 0.28oz; Protein: 0.14oz; Sodium: 5mg; Potassium: 0.0070oz; Phosphorus: 0.0011oz

69. Chinese Beef Wraps

Preparation time: 10 minutes

Cooking time: 30 minutes

Servings: 2

Ingredients:

- 2 iceberg lettuce leaves
- ½ diced cucumber
- 1 teaspoon canola oil
- 5-ounce lean ground beef
- 1 teaspoon ground ginger
- 1 tablespoon chili flakes
- 1 minced garlic clove
- 1 tablespoon rice wine vinegar

Directions:

1. Mix the ground meat with the garlic, rice wine vinegar, chili flakes, and ginger in a bowl. Heat-up oil in a skillet over medium heat.
2. Put the beef in the pan and cook for 20-25 minutes or until cooked through. Serve beef mixture with diced cucumber in each lettuce wrap and fold.

Per serving: Calories: 156kcal; Fat: 0.071oz; Carbs: 0.14oz; Protein: 0.49oz; Sodium: 54mg; Potassium: 0oz; Phosphorus: 0.000035oz

70. Eggplant and Mushroom Sauté

Preparation time: 10 minutes

Cooking time: 30 minutes

Servings: 4

Ingredients:

- 2 pounds oyster mushrooms, chopped
- 6 ounces shallots, peeled, chopped
- 1 yellow onion, chopped
- 2 eggplants, cubed
- 3 celery stalks, chopped
- 1 tablespoon parsley, chopped
- A pinch of sea salt
- Black pepper to taste
- 1 tablespoon savory, dried
- 3 tablespoons coconut oil, melted

Directions:

1. Heat up a pan with the oil over medium high heat, add onion, stir and cook for 4 minutes.
2. Add shallots, stir and cook for 4 more minutes.
3. Add eggplant pieces, mushrooms, celery, savory and black pepper to taste, stir then cook for 15 minutes.
4. Add parsley, stir again, cook for a couple more minutes, divide between plates and serve.
5. Enjoy!

Per serving: Calories: 1013kcal; Fat: 0.38oz; Carbs: 5.52oz; Protein: 2.44oz; Sodium: 105mg; Potassium: 0.0077oz; Phosphorus: 0.0074oz

71. Marinated Shrimp Pasta Salad

Preparation time: 15 minutes

Cooking time: 5 hours

Servings: 1

Ingredients:

- 1/4 cup of honey
- 1/4 cup of balsamic vinegar
- 1/2 of an English cucumber, cubed
- 1/2 pound of fully cooked shrimp
- 15 baby carrots
- 1.5 cups of dime-sized cut cauliflower
- 4 stalks of celery, diced
- 1/2 large yellow bell pepper (diced)
- 1/2 red onion (diced)

- 1/2 large red bell pepper (diced)
- 12 ounces of uncooked tri-color pasta (cooked)
- 3/4 cup of olive oil
- 3 tsp. of mustard (Dijon)
- 1/2 tsp. of garlic (powder)
- 1/2 tsp. pepper

Directions:

1. Cut vegetables and put them in a bowl with the shrimp.
2. Whisk together the honey, balsamic vinegar, garlic powder, pepper, and Dijon mustard in your small bowl. While still whisking, slowly add the oil and whisk it all together.
3. Place the cooked pasta to the bowl with the shrimp and vegetables and mix it.
4. Toss the sauce to coat the pasta, shrimp, and vegetables evenly.
5. Cover and chill for a minimum of five hours before serving. Stir and serve while chilled.

Per serving: Calories: 205kcal; Fat: 0.46oz; Carbs: 0.35oz; Protein: 0.42oz; Sodium: 163mg; Potassium: 0.0055oz; Phosphorus: 0.0038oz

72. Tuna Macaroni Salad

Preparation time: 5 minutes

Cooking time: 25 minutes

Servings: 10 servings

Ingredients:

- 1 1/2 cups uncooked macaroni
- 1 (6 oz.) can of tuna in water
- 1/4 cup mayonnaise
- 2 medium celery stalks, diced
- 1 tbsp. lemon pepper seasoning

Directions:

1. Cook the pasta and let it cool in the refrigerator.
2. Drain the tuna in a colander and rinse it with cold water.
3. Add the tuna and celery once the macaroni has cooled.
4. Stir in mayonnaise and sprinkle with lemon seasoning. Mix well. Serve cold.

Per serving: Calories: 136kcal; Fat: 0.14oz; Carbs: 0.63oz; Protein: 0.28oz; Sodium: 75mg; Potassium: 0.0044oz; Phosphorus: 0.0032oz

73. Spanish Rice

Preparation time: 5 minutes

Cooking time: 20 minutes

Servings: 2

Ingredients:

- White rice – .75 cup
- Chicken broth, low sodium– 1.5 cups
- Onion dehydrated flakes – 2 tablespoons
- Garlic, minced – 2 cloves
- Lemon juice – 1 tablespoon
- Cumin, ground - .25 teaspoon
- Chili powder - .5 teaspoon
- Oregano, dried - .5 teaspoon
- Black pepper, ground - .25 teaspoon
- Cilantro, chopped – 3 tablespoons

Directions:

1. Place the rice, chicken broth, onion flakes, and minced garlic in a medium-sized saucepan. Bring the chicken broth and the rice to a boil in a medium heat, and then reduce the heat to a light simmer, cover it with a lid, and allow it to cook 'til the liquid has all been absorbed about eighteen to twenty minutes.
2. Use your fork to fluff the rice mix in the lemon juice, cumin, chili powder, oregano, black pepper, and cilantro. Once combined, serve the rice while still warm.

Per serving: Calories: 303kcal; Fat: 0.035oz; Carbs: 2.29oz; Protein: 0.21oz; Sodium: 57mg; Potassium: 0.0070oz; Phosphorus: 0.0037oz

74. Chicken & Cauliflower Rice Casserole

Preparation time: 15 minutes

Cooking time: 1 hour & 15 minutes

Servings: 8-10

Ingredients:

- 2 tablespoons coconut oil, divided
- 3-pound bone-in chicken thighs and drumsticks
- Salt
- ground black pepper
- 3 carrots, peeled and sliced
- 1 onion, chopped finely
- 2 garlic cloves, chopped finely

- 2 tablespoons fresh cinnamon, chopped finely
- 2 teaspoons ground cumin
- 1 teaspoon ground coriander
- 12 teaspoon ground cinnamon
- ½ teaspoon ground turmeric
- 1 teaspoon paprika
- ¼ tsp red pepper cayenne
- 1 (28-ounce) can diced Red bell peppers with liquid
- 1 red bell pepper, thin strips
- ½ cup fresh parsley leaves, minced
- Salt, to taste
- 1 head cauliflower, grated to some rice-like consistency
- 1 lemon, sliced thinly

Directions:

1. Warm oven to 375 deg. F. In a large pan, melt 1 tablespoon of coconut oil at high heat. Add chicken pieces and cook for about 3-5 minutes per side or till golden brown.
2. Transfer the chicken to a plate. In a similar pan, sauté the carrot, onion, garlic, and ginger for about 4-5 minutes on medium heat.
3. Stir in spices and remaining coconut oil. Add chicken, Red bell peppers, bell pepper, parsley plus salt, and simmer for approximately 3-5 minutes.
4. In the bottom of a 13x9-inch rectangular baking dish, spread the cauliflower rice evenly. Place chicken mixture over cauliflower rice evenly and top with lemon slices.
5. With foil paper, cover the baking dish and bake for approximately 35 minutes. Uncover the baking dish and bake for about 25 minutes.

Per serving: Calories: 412kcal; Fat: 0.42oz; Carbs: 0.81oz; Protein: 1.20oz; Sodium: 207mg; Potassium: 0.0067oz; Phosphorus: 0.0036oz

75. Baked Flounder

Preparation time: 15 minutes

Cooking time: 5 minutes

Servings: 2

Ingredients:

- 2 (3-oz.) flounder fillets
- 1/4 cup mayonnaise
- Juice of 1 lime

- Zest of 1 lime
- 1/4 cup chopped fresh cilantro
- Ground black pepper to taste

Directions:

1. Preheat the oven to 400 deg. F.
2. Stir the cilantro, lime juice, lime zest, and mayonnaise in a bowl.
3. Prepare the foil on a clean work surface. Place a flounder fillet in the center of each square. Top the fillets evenly with the mayonnaise mixture. Season the flounder with pepper.
4. Fold the foil's sides over the fish and place them on a baking sheet. Bake for 4–5 minutes, unfold the packets, and serve.

Per serving: Calories: 92kcal; Fat: 0.14oz; Carbs: 0.071oz; Protein: 0.42oz; Sodium: 167mg; Potassium: 0.0048oz; Phosphorus: 0.0073oz

76. Oven-Roasted Zucchini With Herbs

Preparation time: 10 minutes

Cooking time: 20 minutes

Servings: 4

Ingredients:

- 4 medium zucchinis, sliced into rounds
- 2 tablespoons olive oil
- 1/2 teaspoon garlic powder
- 1/2 teaspoon dried thyme
- 1/2 teaspoon dried rosemary
- Freshly ground black pepper to taste

Directions:

1. Preheat the oven to 200 degrees C (about 400 degrees F).
2. In a large bowl, combine zucchini rounds, olive oil, garlic powder, thyme, rosemary, and black pepper.
3. Mix well to ensure the zucchini is fully coated with the herbs and oil.
4. Arrange the zucchini in a single layer on a baking sheet lined with parchment paper.
5. Roast in the oven for 20 minutes, or until the zucchini is tender and slightly browned at the edges.
6. Serve warm as a side dish.

Per serving: Calories: 76kcal; Fat: 0.25oz; Carbohydrates: 0.14oz; Protein: 0.035oz; Sodium: 4mg; Potassium: 0.0090oz; Phosphorus: 0.0011oz

77. Asparagus Shrimp Linguini

Preparation time: 10 minutes

Cooking time: 35 minutes

Servings: 1 ½ cup

Ingredients:

- 8 ounces of uncooked linguini
- 1 tablespoon of olive oil
- 1¾ cups of asparagus
- ½ cup of unsalted butter
- 2 garlic cloves
- 3 ounces of cream cheese
- 2 tablespoons of fresh parsley
- ¾ teaspoon of dried basil
- 2/3 cup of dry white wine
- ½ pound of peeled and cooked shrimp

Directions:

1. Preheat oven to 350 deg. F
2. Cook the linguini in boiling water 'til it becomes tender, then drain
3. Place the asparagus on a baking sheet, then spread two tablespoons of oil over the asparagus. Bake for about 7 to 8 minutes or until it is tender
4. Remove baked asparagus from the oven and place it on a plate. Cut the asparagus into pieces of medium-sized once cooled
5. Mince the garlic and chop the parsley
6. Melt ½ cup of butter in a huge skillet with the minced garlic
7. Stir in the cream cheese, mixing as it melts
8. Stir in the parsley and basil, then simmer for about 5 minutes. Mix either in boiling water or dry white wine, stirring until the sauce becomes smooth
9. Add the cooked shrimp and asparagus, then stir and heat until it is evenly warm
10. Toss your cooked pasta with the sauce then serve

Per serving: Calories: 544kcal; Fat: 1.13oz; Carbs: 1.52oz; Protein: 0.74oz; Sodium: 170mg; Potassium: 0.0071oz; Phosphorus: 0.0044oz

78. Breakfast Salad From Grains And Fruits

Preparation time: 5 minutes

Cooking time: 15 minutes

Servings: 6

Ingredients:

- 1 8-oz low fat vanilla yogurt
- 1 mango
- 1 Red delicious apple
- 1 Granny Smith apple
- ¾ cup bulgur
- ¼ teaspoon salt
- 3 cups water

Directions:

1. On high fire, place a large pot and bring water to a boil.
2. Add bulgur and rice. Lower fire to a simmer and cooks for ten minutes while covered.
3. Turn off fire, set aside for 2 minutes while covered.
4. In baking sheet, transfer and evenly spread grains to cool.
5. Meanwhile, peel mango and cut into sections. Chop and core apples.
6. Once grains are cool, transfer to a large serving bowl along with fruits.
7. Add yogurt and mix well to coat.
8. Serve and enjoy.

Per serving: Calories: 187kcal; Fat: 0.21oz; Carbs: 0.14oz; Protein: 0.21oz; Sodium: 117mg; Potassium: 0.0019oz; Phosphorus: 0.0021oz

79. Thai Spiced Halibut

Preparation time: 5 minutes

Cooking time: 20 minutes

Servings: 2 servings

Ingredients:

- 2 tablespoons coconut oil
- 1 cup white rice
- ¼ teaspoon black pepper
- ½ diced red chili
- 1 tablespoon fresh basil
- 2 pressed garlic cloves
- 4 oz. halibut fillet
- 1 halved lime
- 2 sliced green onions
- 1 lime leaf

Directions:

1. Preheat oven to 400 deg. F/Gas Mark 5.

2. Add half of the ingredients into baking paper and fold into a parcel.
3. Repeat for your second parcel.
4. Add to the oven for 15-20 minutes or until fish is thoroughly cooked through.
5. Serve with cooked rice.

Per serving: Calories: 311kcal; Fat: 0.53oz; Carbs: 0.60oz; Protein: 0.56oz; Sodium: 31mg; Potassium: 0.0077oz; Phosphorus: 0.0055oz

80. Chicken And Savory Rice

Preparation time: 15 minutes
Cooking time: 45 minutes
Servings: 4
Ingredients:

- 4 medium chicken breasts
- 1 baby marrow (chopped)
- 1 red bell pepper (chopped)
- 3 tbsp olive oil
- 1 onion
- 1 garlic clove (minced)
- ½ tsp of black pepper
- 1 tbsp of cumin
- ¼ tsp cayenne pepper
- 2 cups of rice

Directions:

1. Add 2 tbsp of olive oil to medium heat and place the chicken breasts into the pan. Cook for 15 minutes and remove from the pan.
2. Place another tbsp of olive oil to the pan, and add the baby marrow, onion, red pepper, and corn.
3. Sauté the vegetables on medium heat for 10 minutes or until golden brown.
4. Add minced garlic, black pepper, cumin, and cayenne pepper to the vegetables. Stir the vegetables and spices together well.
5. Cut the chicken into cube and add it back to the pan. Mix it with the vegetables for 5 minutes.
6. In a medium pot, fill it up with water until it is 2/3 full. Add the rice to the pot then cook it for 35-40 minutes.
7. Serve the chicken and vegetable mixture on a bed of rice with extra black pepper.

Per serving: Calories: 374kcal; Fat: 0.21oz; Carbs: 2.29oz; Protein: 0.53oz; Sodium: 120mg; Potassium: 0.0090oz; Phosphorus: 0.0059oz

81. Tuna Casserole

Preparation time: 15 minutes
Cooking time: 35 minutes
Servings: 4
Ingredients:

- ½ cup cheddar cheese, shredded
- 2 red bell peppers, chopped
- 7 oz. tuna filet, chopped
- 1 teaspoon ground coriander
- ½ teaspoon salt
- 1 teaspoon olive oil
- ½ teaspoon dried oregano

Directions:

1. Brush the casserole mold with olive oil. Mix up together chopped tuna fillet with dried oregano and ground coriander.
2. Place the fish in the mold and flatten well to get the layer. Then add chopped Red bell peppers and shredded cheese. Cover the casserole with foil and secure the edges. Bake the meal for 35 minutes at 355 deg. F. Serve.

Per serving: Calories: 260kcal; Fat: 0.76oz; Carbs: 0.095oz; Protein: 0.52oz; Sodium: 200mg; Potassium: 0.0039oz; Phosphorus: 0.0054oz

82. Ground Beef And Rice Soup

Preparation time: 15 minutes
Cooking time: 40 minutes
Servings: 1
Ingredients:

- ½ pound Extra-lean ground beef
- ½, chopped Small sweet onion
- 1 tsp. Minced garlic
- 2 cups Water
- 1 cup Low-sodium beef broth
- ½ cup, uncooked Long-grain white rice
- 1, chopped Celery stalk
- ½ cup, cut into 1-inch pieces Fresh green beans
- 1 tsp. Chopped fresh thyme

- Ground black pepper

Directions:

1. Sauté the ground beef in a saucepan for 6 minutes or until the beef is completely browned.
2. Drain off the extra fat then add the onion & garlic to the saucepan.
3. Sauté the vegetables for about 3 minutes, or until they are softened.
4. Add the celery, rice, beef broth, and water.
5. Let it boil, lower the heat to low, and simmer for 30 minutes or until the rice is tender.
6. Add the green beans and thyme and simmer for 3 minutes.
7. Take the soup from the heat then season with pepper.

Per serving: Calories: 154kcal; Fat: 0.25oz; Carbs: 0.49oz; Protein: 0.32oz; Sodium: 133mg; Potassium: 0.0063oz; Phosphorus: 0.0027oz

83. Enjoyable Green Lettuce And Bean Medley

Preparation time: 10 minutes

Cooking time: 4 hours

Servings: 4

Ingredients:

- 5 carrots, sliced
- 1 ½ cups great northern beans, dried
- 2 garlic cloves, minced
- 1 yellow onion, chopped
- Pepper to taste
- ½ teaspoon oregano, dried
- 5 ounces baby green lettuce
- 4 ½ cups low sodium veggie stock
- 2 teaspoons lemon peel, grated
- 3 tablespoon lemon juice

Directions:

1. Add beans, onion, carrots, garlic, oregano and stock to your Slow Cooker.
2. Stir well.
3. Place lid and cook on HIGH for 4 hours.
4. Add green lettuce, lemon juice and lemon peel.
5. Stir then let it sit for 5 minutes.
6. Divide between serving platters and enjoy!

Per serving: Calories: 219kcal; Fat: 0.28oz; Carbs: 0.49oz; Protein: 0.28oz; Sodium: 85mg; Potassium: 0.0077oz; Phosphorus: 0.0074oz

84. Hawaiian Chicken Salad

Preparation time: 5 minutes

Cooking time: 30 minutes

Servings: 4

Ingredients:

- 1 1/2 cups of chicken breast, cooked, chopped
- 1 cup pineapple chunks
- 1 1/4 cups lettuce iceberg, shredded
- 1/2 cup celery, diced
- 1/2 cup mayonnaise
- 1/8 tsp (dash) Tabasco sauce
- 2 lemon juice
- 1/4 tsp black pepper

Directions:

1. Combine the cooked chicken, pineapple, lettuce, and celery in a medium bowl. Just set aside.
2. In a small bowl, make the dressing. Mix the mayonnaise, Tabasco sauce, pepper, and lemon juice.
3. Use the chicken mixture to add the dressing and stir until well mixed.

Per serving: Calories: 310kcal; Fat: 0.81oz; Carbs: 0.32oz; Protein: 0.60oz; Sodium: 200mg; Potassium: 0.0092oz; Phosphorus: 0.0047oz

85. Chinese Tempeh Stir Fry

Preparation time: 5 minutes

Cooking time: 15 minutes

Servings: 2 servings

Ingredients:

- 2 oz. sliced tempeh
- 1 cup cooked rice
- 1 minced garlic clove
- ½ cup green onions
- 1 tsp. minced fresh ginger
- 1 tbsp. coconut oil
- ½ cup corn

Directions:

1. Heat the oil in a skillet or wok on a high heat then add the garlic and ginger.
2. Sauté for 1 minute.
3. Now add the tempeh and cook for 5-6 minutes before adding the corn for a further 10 minutes.
4. Now add the green onions and serve over rice.

Per serving: Calories: 304kcal; Fat: 0.14oz; Carbs: 1.23oz; Protein: 0.35oz; Sodium: 91mg; Potassium: 0.0072oz; Phosphorus: 0.0042oz

86. Salmon and Pesto Salad

Preparation time: 5 minutes

Cooking time: 15 minutes

Servings: 2 servings

Ingredients:

For the pesto:

- 1 minced garlic clove
- ½ cup fresh arugula
- ¼ cup extra virgin olive oil
- ½ cup fresh basil
- 1 teaspoon black pepper

For the salmon:

- 4 oz. skinless salmon fillet
- 1 tablespoon coconut oil

For the salad:

- ½ juiced lemon
- 2 sliced radishes
- ½ cup iceberg lettuce
- 1 teaspoon black pepper

Directions:

1. Prepare the pesto by blending all the pesto ingredients in a food processor or by grinding with a pestle and mortar. Set aside.
2. Add a skillet to the stove on medium-high heat and melt the coconut oil.
3. Add the salmon to the pan.
4. Cook for 7-8 minutes and turn over.
5. Cook for a further 3-4 minutes or 'til cooked through.
6. Remove fillets from the skillet and allow to rest.
7. Mix the lettuce and the radishes and squeeze over the juice of ½ lemon.
8. Flake the salmon with a fork then mix through the salad.

9. Toss to coat and sprinkle with a little black pepper to serve.

Per serving: Calories: 221kcal; Fat: 1.20oz; Carbs: 0.035oz; Protein: 0.46oz; Sodium: 80mg; Potassium: 0.0042oz; Phosphorus: 0.0056oz

87. The Kale and Green Lettuce Soup

Preparation time: 5 minutes

Cooking time: 10 minutes

Servings: 4

Ingredients:

- 3 ounces coconut oil
- 8 ounces kale, chopped
- 4 1/3 cups coconut almond milk
- Sunflower seeds and pepper to taste

Directions:

1. Take a skillet then place it over medium heat.
2. Add kale and sauté for 2-3 minutes
3. Add kale to blender.
4. Add water, spices, coconut almond milk to blender as well.
5. Blend until smooth and pour mix into bowl.
6. Serve and enjoy!

Per serving: Calories: 124kcal; Fat: 0.46oz; Carbs: 0.25oz; Protein: 0.15oz; Sodium: 105mg; Potassium: 0.0041oz; Phosphorus: 0.0039oz

88. Cauliflower Rice

Preparation time: 5 minutes

Cooking time: 10 minutes

Servings: 1

Ingredients:

- 1 small head cauliflower cut into florets
- 1 tbsp. butter
- ¼ tsp black pepper
- ¼ tsp garlic powder
- ¼ tsp salt-free herb seasoning blend

Directions:

1. Blitz cauliflower pieces in a food processor until it has a grain-like consistency.
2. Melt butter in a saucepan and add spices.
3. Add the cauliflower rice grains and cook over low-medium heat for approximately 10 minutes.

4. Use your fork to fluff the rice before serving.
5. Serve as an alternative to rice with curries, stews, and starch to accompany meat and fish dishes.

Per serving: Calories: 47kcal; Fat: 0.071oz; Carbs: 0.14oz; Protein: 0.035oz; Sodium: 200mg; Potassium: 0.0037oz; Phosphorus: 0.0011oz

89. Vegetarian Taco Salad

Preparation time: 15 minutes

Cooking time: 15 minutes

Servings: 2

Ingredients:

- 1½ cups canned low-sodium or no-salt-added pinto beans, rinsed and drained
- 1 (10-ounce) package frozen white rice, thawed
- 1 red bell pepper, chopped
- 3 scallions, white and green parts, chopped
- 1 jalapeño pepper, minced
- 1 cup frozen corn, thawed and drained
- 1 tablespoon chili powder
- 1 cup chopped romaine lettuce
- 2 cups chopped butter lettuce
- ½ cup powerhouse salsa
- ½ cup grated pepper jack cheese

Directions:

1. In your medium bowl, combine the beans, rice, bell pepper, scallions, jalapeño, and corn.
2. Sprinkle with the chili powder and stir gently.
3. Stir in the romaine and butter lettuce.
4. Serve topped with Powerhouse Salsa and cheese.

Per serving: Calories: 254kcal; Fat: 0.25oz; Carbs: 1.38oz; Protein: 0.39oz; Sodium: 140mg; Potassium: 0.0070oz; Phosphorus: 0.0049oz

90. Salmon And Green Beans

Preparation time: 10 minutes

Cooking time: 20 minutes

Servings: 4

Ingredients:

- 3 oz x 4 salmon fillets
- ½ lb. of green beans
- 2 tbsp of dill
- 2 tbsp of coriander
- 2 lemons
- 2 tbsp olive oil
- 4 tbsp of mayonnaise

Directions:

1. Rinse and salmon fillets and wait for it to dry. Don't remove the skin.
2. Wash green beans and chop the tips of the green beans.
3. Heat the oven up to 425 deg.-Fahrenheit.
4. Spray an oven sheet pan with cooking spray and place the salmon fillets on the sheet pan.
5. Chop up the dill and combine it with the mayonnaise.
6. Put mayo mixture on top of the salmon fillets.
7. Place the green beans next to the salmon fillets and drizzle olive oil on top of everything.
8. Place the oven baking sheet in the middle of the oven then cook for 15 minutes.
9. Slice the lemons into wedges and serve with the salmon fillets and green beans.

Per serving: Calories: 399kcal; Fat: 0.74oz; Carbs: 0.28oz; Protein: 1.34oz; Sodium: 129mg; Potassium: 0.0071oz; Phosphorus: 0.0079oz

Chapter 5.   Soups

91. Nutmeg Chicken Soup

Preparation time: 10 minutes

Cooking time: 20 minutes

Servings: 4

Ingredients:

- 1 lb. boneless, skinless chicken breasts, uncooked
- 1 1/2 cups onion, sliced
- 1 1/2 cups celery, chopped
- 1 tbsp olive oil
- 1 cup fresh carrots, chopped
- 1 cup fresh green beans, chopped
- 3 tbsp all-purpose white flour
- 1 tsp dried oregano
- 2 tsp dried basil
- 1/4 tsp nutmeg
- 1 tsp thyme
- 32 oz reduced-sodium chicken broth
- 1/2 cup 1% low-fat milk
- 2 cups frozen green peas
- 1/4 tsp black pepper

Directions:

1. Add chicken to a skillet and sauté for 6 minutes then remove it from the heat.
2. Warm up olive oil in a pan then sauté onion for 5 minutes.
3. Stir in green beans, carrots, chicken, basil, oregano, flour, thyme, and nutmeg.
4. Sauté for 3 minutes then transfer the ingredients to a large pan.
5. Add milk and broth and cook until it boils.
6. Stir in green peas then cook for 5 minutes.
7. Adjust seasoning with pepper and serve warm.

Per serving: Calories: 131kcal; Fat: 0.11oz; Carbs: 0.42oz; Protein: 0.49oz; Sodium: 143mg; Potassium: 0.0094oz; Phosphorus: 0.0060oz

92. Green Bean Veggie Stew

Preparation time: 10 minutes

Cooking time: 30-35 minutes

Servings: 1

Ingredients:

- 6 cups shredded green cabbage
- 3 celery stalks, chopped
- 1 teaspoon oil
- ½ large sweet onion, chopped
- 1 teaspoon minced garlic
- 1 scallion, chopped
- 2 tablespoons chopped fresh parsley
- 2 tablespoons lemon juice
- 1 teaspoon chopped fresh oregano
- 1 tablespoon chopped fresh thyme
- 1 teaspoon chopped savory
- Water
- 1 cup fresh green beans, cut into 1" pieces
- Black pepper (ground), to taste

Directions:

1. Take a medium-large cooking pot, heat oil over medium heat.
2. Add onion and stir-cook until it becomes translucent and soft.
3. Add garlic and stir-cook until it becomes fragrant.
4. Add cabbage, celery, scallion, parsley, lemon juice, thyme, savory, and oregano; add water to cover veggies by 3-4 inches.
5. Stir the mixture and boil it.
6. Over low heat, cover, and simmer the mixture for about 25 minutes until veggies are tender.
7. Add green beans and cook for 2-3 more minutes. Season with black pepper to taste. Serve warm.

Per serving: Calories: 56kcal; Fat: 0.035oz; Carbs: 0.25oz; Protein: 0.035oz; Sodium: 31mg; Potassium: 0.0068oz; Phosphorus: 0.0068oz

93. Chicken Wild Rice Soup

Preparation time: 10 minutes

Cooking time: 15 minutes

Servings: 6

Ingredients:

- 2/3 cup wild rice, uncooked
- 1 tbsp onion, chopped finely
- 1 tbsp fresh parsley, chopped
- 1 cup carrots, chopped
- 8 oz chicken breast, cooked
- 2 tbsp oil
- 1/4 cup all-purpose white flour
- 5 cups low-sodium chicken broth
- 1 tbsp slivered almonds

Directions:

1. Start by adding rice and 2 cups broth along with ½ cup water to a cooking pot.
2. Cook 'til the rice is al dente and set it aside.
3. Add oil to a saucepan and melt it.
4. Stir in onion and sauté until soft then add the flour and the remaining broth.
5. Stir then cook for 1 minute then add the chicken, cooked rice, and carrots.
6. Cook for 5 minutes on simmer.
7. Garnish with almonds. Serve fresh.

Per serving: Calories: 287kcal; Fat: 0.25oz; Carbs: 1.23oz; Protein: 0.74oz; Sodium: 182mg; Potassium: 0.010oz; Phosphorus: 0.0077oz

94. Eggplant And Red Pepper Soup

Preparation time: 20 minutes

Cooking time: 40 minutes

Servings: 6

Ingredients:

- Sweet onion – 1 small, cut into quarters
- Small red bell peppers – 2, halved
- Cubed eggplant – 2 cups
- Garlic – 2 cloves, crushed
- Olive oil – 1 Tbsp.
- Chicken stock – 1 cup
- Water
- Chopped fresh basil – ¼ cup
- Ground black pepper

Directions:

1. Preheat the oven to 350 deg. F.
2. Put the onions, red peppers, eggplant, and garlic in a baking dish.
3. Drizzle the vegetables with the olive oil.

4. Roast the vegetables for 30 minutes or 'til they are slightly charred and soft.
5. Cool the vegetables slightly and remove the skin from the peppers.
6. Puree the vegetables with a hand mixer (with the chicken stock).
7. Transfer the soup to a medium pot then add enough water to reach the desired thickness.
8. Heat the soup to a simmer and add the basil.
9. Season with pepper and serve.

Per serving: Calories: 61kcal; Fat: 0.071oz; Carbs: 0.32oz; Protein: 0.071oz; Sodium: 98mg; Potassium: 0.0085oz; Phosphorus: 0.0043oz

95. Hungarian Cherry Soup

Preparation time: 10 minutes

Cooking time: 15 minutes

Servings: 4

Ingredients:

- 1 1/2 cup fresh cherries
- 3 cups water
- 2 cups stevia
- 1/16 tsp salt
- 1 tbsp all-purpose white flour
- 1/2 cup reduced-fat sour cream

Directions:

1. Warm the water in a saucepan and add cherries and stevia.
2. Let it boil then simmer for 10 minutes.
3. Remove 2 tbsp of the cooking liquid and keep it aside.
4. Separate ¼ cup of liquid in a bowl and allow it to cool.
5. Add flour and sour cream to this liquid.
6. Mix well then return the mixture to the saucepan. Cook for 5 minutes on low heat. Garnish the soup with the reserved 2 tbsp of liquid. Serve and enjoy.

Per serving: Calories: 144kcal; Fat: 0.14oz; Carbs: 0.88oz; Protein: 0.071oz; Sodium: 57mg; Potassium: 0.0051oz; Phosphorus: 0.0014oz

96. Soup with Leek, Spinach, and Chicken

Preparation Time: 10 minutes

Cooking Time: 15 minutes

Servings: 4

Ingredients:

- 3 tbsp of butter, without salt
- 2 leeks, sliced thinly, white parts only
- 4 cups of tender baby spinach
- 4 cups of broth made from chicken
- 1 tsp of salt
- 1/4 tsp of black pepper, freshly ground
- 2 cups of chicken, pulled from a cooked rotisserie chicken
- 1 tbsp of chives, freshly cut into thin slices
- 2 tsp of lemon peel, finely grated or minced

Directions:

1. Heat a large soup pot over a high flame and melt the butter.
2. Toss in the leeks, cooking until they are soft and starting to take on a golden color, about 3 to 5 minutes.
3. Introduce the spinach, chicken stock, salt, and black pepper to the pot, and bring the mixture to a boil.
4. Reduce the flame to simmer and let the soup cook just until the spinach has wilted, which should take about 1 to 2 minutes.
5. Add the shredded chicken to the soup, continuing to cook until the chicken is thoroughly heated, another 1 to 2 minutes.
6. Garnish the soup with chives and lemon zest before serving it warm.

Per Serving: Calories: 256kcal; Fat: 0.42oz; Carbs: 0.32oz; Protein: 0.95oz; Sodium: 183mg; Potassium: 0.0084oz; Phosphorus: 0.0067oz

97. Classic Chicken Soup

Preparation time: 5-10 minutes

Cooking time: 35 minutes

Servings: 1

Ingredients:

- 2 teaspoons minced garlic
- 2 celery stalks, chopped
- 1 tablespoon oil
- ½ sweet onion, diced
- 1 carrot, diced
- 4 cups water

- 1 teaspoon chopped fresh thyme
- 2 cups chopped cooked chicken breast
- 1 cup chicken stock
- Black pepper (ground), to taste
- 2 tablespoons chopped fresh parsley

Directions:

1. Take a medium-large cooking pot, heat oil over medium heat.
2. Add onion and stir-cook until it becomes translucent and softened.
3. Add garlic and stir-cook until it becomes fragrant.
4. Add celery, carrot, chicken, chicken stock, and water. Boil the mixture.
5. Over low heat simmers the mixture for about 25-30 minutes until veggies are tender.
6. Mix in thyme and cook for 2 minutes. Season to taste with black pepper.
7. Serve warm with parsley on top.

Per serving: Calories: 135kcal; Fat: 0.21oz; Carbs: 0.11oz; Protein: 0.53oz; Sodium: 74mg; Potassium: 0.0073oz; Phosphorus: 0.0043oz

98. Mediterranean Vegetable Soup

Preparation time: 5 minutes

Cooking time: 30 minutes

Servings: 4

Ingredients:

- 1 tbsp. oregano
- 2 minced garlic cloves
- 1 tsp. black pepper
- 1 diced zucchini
- 1 cup diced eggplant
- 4 cups water
- 1 diced red pepper
- 1 tbsp. extra-virgin olive oil
- 1 diced red onion

Directions:

1. Soak the vegetables in warm water prior to use.
2. In a huge pot, add the oil, chopped onion and minced garlic.
3. Simmer for 5 minutes on low heat.
4. Add the other vegetables to the onions and cook for 7-8 minutes.

5. Place the stock to the pan then bring to a boil on high heat.
6. Stir in the herbs, reduce the heat, and simmer for a further 20 minutes or until thoroughly cooked through.
7. Season with pepper to serve.

Per serving: Calories: 152kcal; Fat: 0.11oz; Carbs: 0.21oz; Protein: 0.035oz; Sodium: 3mg; Potassium: 0.0081oz; Phosphorus: 0.0016oz

99. Delicious Curried Chicken Soup

Preparation time: 10 minutes

Cooking time: 35 minutes

Servings: 10

Ingredients:

- 5 cups cooked chicken, chopped
- 1/4 cup fresh parsley, chopped
- 1/2 cup sour cream
- 1/4 cup apple cider
- 3 cups celery, chopped
- 1 1/2 tbsp. curry powder
- 10 cups chicken broth
- Pepper
- Salt

Directions:

1. Add all ingredients except sour cream and parsley into the stockpot and stir well.
2. Bring to boil over medium-high heat.
3. Turn heat to medium and simmer for 30 minutes.
4. Add parsley and sour cream and stir well.
5. Season with pepper and salt.
6. Serve and enjoy.

Per serving: Calories: 180kcal; Fat: 0.22oz; Carbs: 0.13oz; Protein: 1.02oz; Sodium: 75mg; Potassium: 0.0038oz; Phosphorus: 0.0056oz

100. Pumpkin, Coconut and Sage Soup

Preparation Time: 10 minutes

Cooking Time: 30 minutes

Servings: 3

Ingredients:

- 1 cup of canned pumpkin puree
- 6 cups of chicken stock

- 1 cup of coconut almond milk, low-fat variety
- 1 teaspoon of fresh sage, finely chopped
- 3 cloves of garlic, left whole
- Sunflower seeds and freshly ground pepper, to taste

Directions:

1. In a large pot, combine the canned pumpkin, chicken stock, whole garlic cloves, and chopped sage. Exclude the coconut almond milk for now.
2. Set the pot on a stove over medium heat and bring the mixture to a boil.
3. Once boiling, lower the heat to achieve a gentle simmer and let it cook uncovered for 30 minutes, allowing the flavors to meld together.
4. After 30 minutes, incorporate the coconut almond milk into the soup, stirring well to combine everything evenly.
5. Warm through, then taste and adjust seasoning with freshly ground pepper and add sunflower seeds for a bit of crunch right before serving.
6. Serve hot and savor the creamy, aromatic blend.

Per Serving: Calories: 145kcal; Fat: 0.42oz; Carbs: 0.28oz; Protein: 0.21oz; Sodium: 75mg; Potassium: 0.0041oz; Phosphorus: 0.0039oz

101. Squash and Turmeric Soup

Preparation time: 10 minutes

Cooking time: 30 minutes

Servings: 2

Ingredients:

- 4 cups low-sodium vegetable broth
- 2 medium zucchini squash, peeled and diced
- 2 medium yellow crookneck squash, peeled and diced
- 1 small onion, diced
- 1/2 cup frozen green peas
- 2 tbsp olive oil
- 1/2 cup plain nonfat Greek yogurt
- 2 tsp turmeric

Directions:

1. Warm the broth in a saucepan on medium heat.
2. Toss in onion, squash, and zucchini.
3. Let it simmer for approximately 25 minutes, then add oil and green peas.
4. Cook for another 5 minutes, then allow it to cool.

5. Puree the soup using a handheld blender, then add Greek yogurt and turmeric.
6. Refrigerate it overnight and serve fresh.

Per serving: Calories: 100kcal; Fat: 0.18oz; Carbs: 0.35oz; Protein. 0.14oz, Sodium. 179mg; Potassium: 0.0072oz; Phosphorus: 0.0049oz

102. Thai Chicken Soup

Preparation time: 10 minutes

Cooking time: 30 minutes

Servings: 6

Ingredients:

- 4 chicken breasts, slice into 1/4-inch strips
- 1 tbsp. fresh basil, chopped
- 1 tsp ground ginger
- 1 oz. fresh lime juice
- 1 tbsp. coconut aminos
- 2 tbsp. chili garlic paste
- 1/4 cup fish sauce
- 28 oz. water
- 14 oz. chicken broth
- 14 oz. coconut almond milk

Directions:

1. Add coconut almond milk, basil, ginger, lime juice, coconut aminos, chili garlic paste, fish sauce, water, and broth into the stockpot. Stir well and bring to boil over medium-high heat.
2. Add chicken and stir well. Turn heat to medium-low then simmer for 30 minutes.
3. Stir well and serve.

Per serving: Calories: Calories: 357kcal; Fat: 0.83oz; Carbs: 0.19oz; Protein: 1.12oz; Sodium: 75mg; Potassium: 0.0041oz; Phosphorus: 0.0039oz

103. Paprika Pork Soup

Preparation time: 5 minutes

Cooking time: 35 minutes

Servings: 2

Ingredients:

- 4-ounce sliced pork loin
- 1 teaspoon black pepper
- 2 minced garlic cloves
- 3 cups water

- 1 tablespoon extra-virgin olive oil
- 1 chopped onion
- 1 tablespoon paprika

Directions:

1. Add in the oil, chopped onion and minced garlic.
2. Sauté for 5 minutes on low heat.
3. Add the pork slices to the onions and cook for 7-8 minutes or until browned.
4. Add the water to the pan then bring to a boil on high heat.
5. Reduce heat then simmer for 20 minutes or 'til pork is thoroughly cooked.
6. Season with pepper to serve.

Per serving: Calories: 165kcal; Fat: 0.32oz; Carbs: 0.35oz; Protein: 0.46oz; Sodium: 169mg; Potassium: 0.0101oz; Phosphorus: 0.0056oz

104. Chicken Noodle Soup

Preparation time: 10 minutes

Cooking time: 25 minutes

Servings: 2

Ingredients:

- 1 1/2 cups low-sodium vegetable broth
- 1 cup of water
- 1/4 tsp poultry seasoning
- 1/4 tsp black pepper
- 1 cup chicken strips
- 1/4 cup carrot
- 2 oz. egg noodles, uncooked

Directions:

1. Cook soup on high heat for 25 minutes in a slow cooker.
2. Serve warm.

Per serving: Calories: 103kcal; Fat: 0.11oz; Carbs: 0.39oz; Protein: 0.28oz; Sodium: 255mg; Potassium: 0.0093oz; Phosphorus: 0.0045oz

105. Wild Rice Asparagus Soup

Preparation time: 10 minutes

Cooking time: 30 minutes

Servings: 4

Ingredients:

- 3/4 cup wild rice

- 2 cups asparagus, chopped
- 1 cup carrots, diced
- 1/2 cup onion, diced
- 3 garlic cloves, minced
- 1/4 cup oil
- 1/2 tsp thyme
- 1/2 tsp fresh ground pepper
- 1/4 tsp nutmeg
- 1 bay leaf
- 1/2 cup all-purpose flour
- 4 cups low-sodium chicken broth
- 1/2 cup extra dry vermouth
- 2 cups cooked chicken
- 4 cups unsweetened almond milk, unenriched

Directions:

1. Cook the wild rice as per the cooking instructions on the box or bag and drain.
2. Melt the oil in a Dutch oven and sauté garlic and onion.
3. Once soft, add spices, herbs, and carrots.
4. Cook on medium heat right until veggies are tender then add flour and stir cook for 10 minutes on low heat.
5. Add 4 cups of broth and vermouth and blend using a handheld blender.
6. Dice the chicken pieces and add asparagus and chicken to the soup.
7. Stir in almond milk and cook for 20 minutes.
8. Add the wild rice and serve warm.

Per serving: Calories: 295kcal; Fat: 0.39oz; Carbs: 0.99oz; Protein: 0.74oz; Sodium: 285mg; Potassium: 0.0080oz; Phosphorus: 0.0054oz

106. Spicy Chicken Soup

Preparation time: 10 minutes

Cooking time: 5 minutes

Servings: 4

Ingredients:

- 2 cups cooked chicken, shredded
- 1/2 cup half and half
- 4 cups chicken broth
- 1/3 cup hot sauce
- 3 tbsp. butter
- 4 oz. cream cheese
- Pepper
- Salt

Directions:

1. Add half and half, broth, hot sauce, butter, and cream cheese into the blender and blend until smooth.
2. Pour blended mixture into the saucepan and cook over medium heat until just hot.
3. Add chicken stir well. Season soup with pepper and salt.
4. Serve and enjoy.

Per serving: Calories: 361kcal; Fat: 0.90oz; Carbs: 0.12oz; Protein: 1.00oz; Sodium: 75mg; Potassium: 0.0041oz; Phosphorus: 0.0039oz

107. Cabbage Turkey Soup

Preparation time: 10 minutes

Cooking time: 40-45 minutes

Servings: 2

Ingredients:

- ½ cup shredded green cabbage
- ½ cup bulgur
- 2 dried bay leaves
- 2 tablespoons chopped fresh parsley
- 1 teaspoon chopped fresh sage
- 1 teaspoon chopped fresh thyme
- 1 celery stalk, chopped
- 1 carrot, sliced thin
- ½ sweet onion, chopped
- 1 teaspoon minced garlic
- 1 teaspoon olive oil
- ½ pound cooked ground turkey, 93% lean
- 4 cups water
- 1 cup chicken stock
- Pinch red pepper flakes
- Black pepper (ground), to taste

Directions:

1. Take a large saucepan or cooking pot, and add oil. Heat over medium heat.
2. Add turkey and stir-cook for 4-5 minutes until evenly brown.
3. Add onion and garlic, and sauté for about 3 minutes to soften the veggies.
4. Add water, chicken stock, cabbage, bulgur, celery, carrot, and bay leaves.

5. Boil the mixture.

6. Over low heat, cover and simmer the mixture for about 30-35 minutes until the bulgur is cooked well and tender.

7. Remove bay leaves. Add parsley, sage, thyme, and red pepper flakes; stir the mixture and season with black pepper. Serve warm.

Per serving: Calories: 83kcal; Fat: 0.14oz; Carbs: 0.071oz; Protein: 0.28oz; Sodium: 63mg; Potassium: 0.0065oz; Phosphorus: 0.0032oz

108. Amazing Zucchini Soup

Preparation time: 10 minutes

Cooking time: 20 minutes

Servings: 4

Ingredients:

- 1 onion, chopped
- 3 zucchinis, cut into medium chunks
- 2 tablespoons coconut almond milk
- 2 garlic cloves, minced
- 4 cups chicken stock
- 2 tablespoons coconut oil
- Pinch of salt
- Black pepper to taste

Directions:

1. Take a pot and place over medium heat.
2. Add oil and let it heat up.
3. Add zucchini, garlic, onion and stir.
4. Cook for 5 minutes.
5. Add stock, salt, pepper and stir.
6. Bring to a boil then lower the heat.
7. Simmer for 20 minutes.
8. Remove from heat and add coconut almond milk.
9. Use an immersion blender until smooth.
10. Ladle into soup bowls and serve.
11. Enjoy!

Per serving: Calories: 160kcal; Fat: 0.071oz; Carbs: 0.14oz; Protein: 0.25oz; Sodium: 75mg; Potassium: 0.0041oz; Phosphorus: 0.0039oz

109. Simple Cabbage Soup

Preparation time: 20 minutes

Cooking time: 35 minutes

Servings: 8

Ingredients:

- 1 tablespoon olive oil
- ½ sweet onion, chopped
- 2 teaspoons minced garlic
- 6 cups of water
- 1 cup sodium-free chicken stock
- ½ head green cabbage, shredded
- 2 carrots, diced
- Freshly ground black pepper
- 2 tablespoons chopped fresh thyme

Directions:

1. Prepare olive oil in a large saucepan over medium-high heat.
2. Sauté the onion and garlic until softened.
3. Add water, chicken stock, cabbage, carrots Let it bring it to a boil.
4. In medium-low heat, simmer the vegetables for 30 minutes or until tender.
5. Season the soup with black pepper. Serve hot, topped with the thyme.

Per serving: Calories: 62kcal; Fat: 0.071oz; Carbs: 0.21oz; Protein: 0.071oz; Sodium: 61mg; Potassium: 0.0071oz; Phosphorus: 0.0011oz

110. Beef Okra Soup

Preparation time: 10 minutes

Cooking time: 45-55 minutes

Servings: 2

Ingredients:

- ½ cup okra
- ½ teaspoon basil
- ½ cup carrots, diced
- 3 ½ cups water
- 1-pound beef stew meat
- 1 cup raw sliced onions
- ½ cup green peas
- 1 teaspoon black pepper
- ½ teaspoon thyme
- ½ cup corn kernels

Directions:

1. Take a medium-large cooking pot and heat oil over medium heat.

2. Add water, beef stew meat, black pepper, onions, basil, thyme, and stir-cook for 40-45 minutes until meat is tender.

3. Add all veggies. Over low heat, simmer the mixture for about 20-25 minutes. Add more water if needed.

4. Serve soup warm.

Per serving: Calories: Calories: 187kcal; Fat: 0.42oz; Carbs: 0.25oz; Protein: 0.39oz; Sodium: 59mg; Potassium: 0.0102oz; Phosphorus: 0.0042oz

Chapter 6.   Meat Main Courses

111. Ground Chicken with Basil

Preparation time: 15 minutes

Cooking time: 16 minutes

Servings: 8

Ingredients:

- 2 pounds lean ground chicken
- 3 tablespoons coconut oil, divided
- 1 zucchini, chopped
- 1 red bell pepper, seeded and chopped
- ½ of green bell pepper, seeded and chopped
- 4 garlic cloves, minced
- 1 (1-inch) piece fresh ginger, minced
- 1 (1-inch) piece fresh turmeric, minced
- 1 fresh red chili, sliced thinly
- 1 tablespoon organic honey
- 1 tablespoon coconut aminos
- 1½ tablespoons fish sauce
- ½ cup fresh basil, chopped
- Salt
- Ground black pepper
- 1 tablespoon fresh lime juice

Directions:

1. Heat a large skillet on medium-high heat. Add ground beef and cook for approximately 5 minutes or till browned completely.
2. Transfer the beef to a bowl. In a similar pan, melt 1 tablespoon of coconut oil on medium-high heat. Add zucchini and bell peppers and stir fry for around 3-4 minutes.
3. Transfer the vegetables inside the bowl with chicken. In precisely the same pan, melt remaining coconut oil on medium heat. Add garlic, ginger, turmeric, and red chili and sauté for approximately 1-2 minutes.
4. Add chicken mixture, honey, and coconut aminos and increase the heat to high. Cook within 4-5 minutes or till sauce is nearly reduced. Stir in remaining ingredients and take off from the heat.

Per serving: Calories: 407kcal; Fat: 0.25oz; Carbs: 0.71oz; Protein: 1.27oz; Sodium: 21.3mg; Potassium: 0.0073oz; Phosphorus: 0.0053oz

112. Herby Beef Stroganoff and Fluffy Rice

Preparation time: 15 minutes

Cooking time: 5 hours

Servings: 6

Ingredients:

- ½ cup onion
- 2 garlic cloves
- 9 ounces of flat-cut beef brisket, cut into 1" cubes
- ½ cup of reduced-sodium beef stock
- 1/3 cup red wine
- ½ teaspoon dried oregano
- ¼ teaspoon freshly ground black pepper
- ½ teaspoon dried thyme
- ½ teaspoon of saffron
- ½ cup almond milk (unenriched)
- ¼ cup all-purpose flour
- 1 cup of water
- 2 ½ cups of white rice

Directions:

1. Dice the onion, then mince the garlic cloves. Mix the beef, stock, wine, onion, garlic, oregano, pepper, thyme, and saffron in your slow cooker.
2. Cover and cook on high within 4-5 hours. Combine the almond milk, flour, and water. Whisk together until smooth.
3. Place the flour mixture to the slow cooker. Cook for another 15 to 25 minutes 'til the stroganoff is thick.
4. Cook the rice using the package instructions, leaving out the salt. Drain off the excess water. Serve the stroganoff over the rice.

Per serving: Calories: 241kcal; Fat: 0.18oz; Carbs: 1.02oz; Protein: 0.53oz; Sodium: 182mg; Potassium: 0.0073oz; Phosphorus: 0.0053oz

113. Roasted Chicken Breast

Preparation time: 15 minutes

Cooking time: 40 minutes

Servings: 4-6

Ingredients:

- ½ of a small apple, peeled, cored, and chopped
- 1 bunch scallion, trimmed and chopped roughly
- 8 fresh ginger slices, chopped
- 2 garlic cloves, chopped
- 3 tablespoons essential olive oil
- 12 teaspoon sesame oil, toasted
- 3 tablespoons using apple cider vinegar
- 1 tablespoon fish sauce
- 1 tablespoon coconut aminos
- Salt
- ground black pepper
- 4-pounds chicken thighs

Directions:

1. Pulse all the fixing except chicken thighs in a blender. Transfer a combination and chicken right into a large Ziploc bag and seal it.
2. Shake the bag to marinade well. Refrigerate to marinate for about 12 hours. Warm oven to 400 deg. F. arranges a rack in foil paper-lined baking sheet.
3. Place the chicken thighs on the rack, skin-side down. Roast for about 40 minutes, flipping once within the middle way.

Per serving: Calories: 451kcal; Fat: 0.60oz; Carbs: 9.77oz; Protein: 1.48oz; Sodium: 283mg; Potassium: 0.0044oz; Phosphorus: 0.0043oz

114. Curried Chicken With Cauliflower

Preparation time: 20 minutes

Cooking time: 2 hours and 30 minutes

Servings: 6

Ingredients:

- Lime juice 2 limes
- 1/2 tsp. dried oregano
- Cauliflower head, cut into florets
- 4 tsp. EVOO, divided
- 6 chicken thighs, bone-in
- 1/2 tsp. pepper, divided
- 1/4 tsp. paprika
- 1/2 tsp. ground cumin
- 3 tbsp. curry powder

Directions:

1. Mix a quarter of a tsp. of pepper, paprika, cumin, and curry in a small bowl.
2. Place the chicken thighs to a medium bowl then drizzle with 2 tsp. of olive oil and sprinkle in the curry mixture.
3. Toss them together so that the chicken is well coated.
4. Cover this up and refrigerate it for at least 2 hours.
5. Now set your oven to 400 deg. F.
6. Toss the cauliflower, remaining oil, and the oregano together in a medium bowl. Arrange the cauliflower and chicken across a baking sheet in one layer.
7. Allow this to bake for 40 minutes. Stir the cauliflower and flip the chicken once during the cooking time. The chicken should be browned, and the juices should run clear. The temperature of the chicken must reach 165 deg. F.
8. Serve with some lime juice. Enjoy!

Per serving: Calories: 175kcal; Fat: 0.21oz; Carbs: 0.81oz; Protein: 0.56oz; Sodium: 77mg; Potassium: 0.0101oz; Phosphorus: 0.0054oz

115. Creamy Turkey

Preparation time: 12minutes

Cooking time: 10minutes

Servings: 4

Ingredients:

- 4 skinless, boneless turkey breast halves
- Salt and pepper to taste
- ½ teaspoon ground black pepper
- ½ teaspoon garlic powder
- 1 (10.75 ounces) can chicken soup

Directions:

1. Preheat oven to 375 deg. F.
2. Clean turkey breasts and season with salt, pepper and garlic powder (or whichever seasonings you prefer) on both sides of turkey pieces.
3. Bake for 25 minutes, then add chicken soup then bake for 10 more minutes (or until done). Serve over rice or egg noodles.

Per serving: Calories: 160kcal; Fat: 0oz; Carbs: 0oz; Protein: 0.90oz; Sodium: 157mg; Potassium: 0.0054oz; Phosphorus: 0.0030oz

116. Grilled Chicken

Preparation time: 15 minutes

Cooking time: 41 minutes

Servings: 8

Ingredients:

- 1 (3-inch) piece fresh ginger, minced
- 6 small garlic cloves, minced
- 1½ tablespoons tamarind paste
- 1 tablespoon organic honey
- ¼ cup coconut aminos
- 2½ tablespoons extra virgin olive oil
- 1½ tablespoons sesame oil, toasted
- ½ teaspoon ground cardamom
- Salt
- ground white pepper
- 1 (4-5-pound) whole chicken, cut into 8 pieces

Directions:

1. Mix all ingredients except chicken pieces in a large glass bowl. With a fork, pierce the chicken pieces thoroughly.
2. Add chicken pieces in bowl and coat with marinade generously. Cover and refrigerate to marinate for approximately a couple of hours to overnight.
3. Preheat the grill to medium heat. Grease the grill grate. Place the chicken pieces on the grill, bone-side down. Grill, covered approximately 20-25 minutes.
4. Change the side and grill, covered approximately 6-8 minutes. Change alongside it and grill, covered for about 5-8 minutes. Serve.

Per serving: Calories: 423kcal; Fat: 0.42oz; Carbs: 0.71oz; Protein: 1.48oz; Sodium: 282mg; Potassium: 0oz; Phosphorus: 0oz

117. Beer Pork Ribs

Preparation time: 10 minutes

Cooking time: 8 hours

Servings: 1

Ingredients:

- 2 pounds of pork ribs, cut into two units/racks
- 18 oz. of root beer
- 2 cloves of garlic, minced
- 2 tbsp. of onion powder
- 2 tbsp. of vegetable oil (optional)

Directions:

1. Wrap the pork ribs with vegetable oil and place one unit on the bottom of your slow cooker with half of the minced garlic and the onion powder.
2. Place the other rack on top with the rest of the garlic and onion powder.
3. Pour over the root beer and cover the lid.
4. Let simmer for 8 hours on low heat.
5. Take off and finish optionally in a grilling pan for a nice sear.

Per serving: Calories: 301kcal; Fat: 0.63oz; Carbs: 1.27oz; Protein: 0.74oz; Sodium: 229mg; Potassium: 0.0035oz; Phosphorus: 0.0038oz

118. Chicken Breast And Bok Choy

Preparation time: 10 minutes

Cooking time: 30 minutes

Servings: 4

Ingredients:

- 4 slices lemon
- Pepper, to taste
- 4 chicken breasts, boneless and skinless
- 1 tbsp. Dijon mustard
- 1 small leek, thinly sliced
- 2 julienned carrots
- 2 cups thinly sliced bok choy
- 1 tbsp. chopped thyme
- 1 tbsp. EVOO

Directions:

1. Start by setting your oven to 425 deg. F.
2. Mix the thyme, olive oil, and mustard in a small bowl.
3. Take four 18 inch long pieces of parchment paper and fold them in half. Cut them like you would make a heart. Open each of the pieces and lay them flat.
4. In each parchment piece, place .5 cup of bok choy, a few slices of leek, and a small handful of carrots.
5. Lay the chicken breast on top and season with some pepper.

6. Brush the chicken breasts with the marinade and top each one with a slice of lemon.

7. Fold the packets up, and roll down the edges to seal the packages.

8. Allow them to cook for 20 minutes. Let them rest of 5 minutes, and make sure you open them carefully when serving. Enjoy!

Per serving: Calories: 164kcal; Fat: 0.11oz; Carbs: 0.74oz; Protein: 0.85oz; Sodium: 256mg; Potassium: 0.0067oz; Phosphorus: 0.0009oz

119. Spicy Lamb Curry

Preparation time: 15 minutes

Cooking time: 2 hours 15 minutes

Servings: 6-8

Ingredients:

- 4 teaspoons ground coriander
- 4 teaspoons ground cumin
- ¾ teaspoon ground ginger
- 2 teaspoons ground cinnamon
- ½ teaspoon ground cloves
- ½ teaspoon ground cardamom
- 2 tablespoons sweet paprika
- ½ tablespoon cayenne pepper
- 2 teaspoons chili powder
- 2 teaspoons salt
- 1 tablespoon coconut oil
- 2 pounds boneless lamb, trimmed and cubed into 1-inch size
- Salt
- Ground black pepper
- 2 cups onions, chopped
- 1¼ cups water
- 1 cup of coconut almond milk

Directions:

1. For spice mixture in a bowl, mix all spices. Keep aside. Season the lamb with salt & black pepper.

2. Warm oil on medium-high heat in a large Dutch oven. Add lamb and stir fry for around 5 minutes. Add onion and cook approximately 4-5 minutes.

3. Stir in the spice mixture and cook approximately 1 minute. Add water and coconut almond milk and provide some boil on high heat.

4. Adjust the heat to low and simmer, covered for approximately 1-120 minutes or until the lamb's

desired doneness. Uncover and simmer for about 3-4 minutes. Serve hot.

Per serving: Calories: 466kcal; Fat: 0.35oz; Carbs: 0.81oz; Protein: 1.27oz; Sodium: 203mg; Potassium: 0.0070oz; Phosphorus: 0oz

120. Pork Tenderloin with Roasted Fruit

Preparation time: 15 minutes

Cooking time: 25 minutes

Servings: 2

Ingredients:

- 1 tbsp extra-virgin olive oil
- 1/2 chopped red onion
- 1 pear, seeded & cut into ½-inch wedges
- 1/2 (12-oz) pork tenderloin, cut into 1-inch strips
- 1/8 tsp salt
- 1/8 tsp freshly ground black pepper
- 3/4 cup red grapes
- 1/2 tsp dried thyme leaves

Directions:

1. Preheat the oven to 400 deg. F.

2. Drizzle the olive oil onto a rimmed baking sheet. Add the onion and pears; toss to coat. Roast for 10 minutes.

3. Remove the pan and add the pork. Sprinkle with salt and pepper. Add the grapes and sprinkle everything with the thyme; stir gently.

4. Arrange the fruit and pork in a single layer. Roast, uncovered, stirring gently once during cooking time, for 13 to 18 minutes or until the fruit is tender. Stir well and serve.

Per serving: Calories: 283kcal; Fat: 0.35oz; Carbs: 0.95oz; Protein: 0.81oz; Sodium: 128mg; Potassium: 0.0075oz; Phosphorus: 0.0056oz

121. Teriyaki Beef Skewers

Preparation time: 15 minutes

Cooking time: 10 minutes

Servings: 4

Ingredients:

- 1 lb beef sirloin, cut into cubes
- Low-sodium teriyaki sauce
- Pineapple chunks
- Bell peppers, cut into chunks

- Red onion, cut into chunks
- Olive oil
- Salt and pepper, to taste

Directions:

1. In a bowl, marinate the beef cubes in low-sodium teriyaki sauce for at least 30 minutes.
2. Preheat the grill to medium-high heat.
3. Thread the marinated beef, pineapple chunks, bell peppers, and red onion onto skewers, alternating between them.
4. Brush the skewers with olive oil then season with salt and pepper.
5. Grill the skewers for about 8-10 mins, turning occasionally, 'til the beef is cooked to your desired level of doneness.
6. Remove from the grill then let them rest for a few minutes before serving.

Per serving: Calories: 250kcal; Fat: 0.35oz; Carbs: 0.35oz; Protein: 1.06oz; Sodium: 150mg; Potassium: 0.0071oz; Phosphorus: 0.0035oz

122. Herb-Roasted Lamb Chops

Preparation time: 10 minutes

Cooking time: 20 minutes

Servings: 4

Ingredients:

- 8 lamb chops
- 2 tablespoons olive oil
- 2 cloves garlic, minced
- 1 teaspoon dried rosemary
- 1 teaspoon dried thyme
- Salt and pepper to taste

Directions:

1. Preheat the oven to 400 deg. F.
2. In your small bowl, combine olive oil, minced garlic, dried rosemary, dried thyme, salt, & pepper.
3. Coat the lamb chops evenly by rubbing them with the mixture of olive oil.
4. Bring the lamb chops on a baking sheet lined with parchment paper.
5. Cook the roast in the oven that has been preheated for approximately 15 to 20 minutes, or until the lamb chops reach the desired doneness (145 deg. F for medium-rare).

6. Remove from the oven then let the lamb chops rest for a few minutes before serving.

Per serving: Calories: 290kcal; Fat: 0.74oz; Carbs: 0oz; Protein: 0.85oz; Sodium: 65mg; Potassium: 0.0085oz; Phosphorus: 0.0067oz

123. Beef Brisket

Preparation time: 10 minutes

Cooking time: 3 1/2 hours

Servings: 6

Ingredients:

- 12 ounces trimmed chuck roast
- 2 cloves garlic
- 1 tablespoon thyme
- 1 tablespoon rosemary
- 1 tablespoon mustard
- 1/4 cup extra virgin olive oil
- 1 teaspoon black pepper
- 1 diced onion
- 1 cup, peeled and sliced carrots
- 2 cups low salt stock

Directions:

1. Preheat the oven to 300 deg. F.
2. Soak vegetables in warm water.
3. Make a paste by mixing together the thyme, mustard, rosemary, and garlic. Then mix in the oil and pepper.
4. Add the beef to the dish.
5. Pour the mixture over the beef into a dish.
6. Place the vegetables onto the bottom of the baking dish around the beef.
7. Cover and roast for 3 hours, or until tender.
8. Uncover the dish and continue to cook for 30 minutes in the oven.
9. Serve.

Per serving: Calories: 303kcal; Fat: 0.88oz; Carbs: 0.25oz; Protein: 0.63oz; Sodium: 44mg; Potassium: 0.0087oz; Phosphorus: 0.0097oz

124. Peppercorn Pork Chops

Preparation time: 30 min

Cooking time: 30 minutes

Servings: 4

Ingredients:

- 1 tablespoon crushed black peppercorns
- 4 pork loin chops
- 2 tablespoons olive oil
- 1/4 cup butter
- 5 garlic cloves
- 1 cup green and red bell peppers
- 1/2 cup pineapple juice

Directions:

1. Sprinkle then press peppercorns into both sides of pork chops.
2. Heat oil, butter and garlic cloves in a huge skillet over medium heat, stirring frequently.
3. Place pork chops then cook uncovered for 5–6 minutes.
4. Dice the bell peppers. Place the bell peppers and pineapple juice to the pork chops.
5. Cover then simmer for another 5–6 minutes or 'til pork is thoroughly cooked.

Per serving: Calories: 317kcal; Fat: 0.91oz; Carbs: 0.32oz; Protein: 0.47oz; Sodium: 126mg; Potassium: 0.0088oz; Phosphorus: 0.0041oz

125. Pork Loins with Leeks

Preparation time: 10 minutes

Cooking time: 35 minutes

Servings: 2

Ingredients:

- 1 sliced leek
- 1 tablespoon mustard seeds
- 6-ounce pork tenderloin
- 1 tablespoon cumin seeds
- 1 tablespoon dry mustard
- 1 tablespoon extra-virgin oil

Directions:

1. Preheat the broiler to medium-high heat. In a dry skillet, heat mustard and cumin seeds until they start to pop (3-5 minutes). Grind seeds using a pestle and mortar or blender and then mix in the dry mustard.
2. Massage the pork on all sides using the mustard blend and add to a baking tray to broil for 25-30 minutes or until cooked through. Turn once halfway through.

3. Remove and place to one side, then heat-up the oil in a pan in a medium heat then add the leeks for 5-6 minutes or until soft. Serve the pork tenderloin on a bed of leeks and enjoy it!

Per serving: Calories: 139kcal; Fat: 0.18oz; Carbs: 0.071oz; Protein: 0.63oz; Sodium: 47mg; Potassium: 0.0016oz; Phosphorus: 0.0098oz

126. Beef Brochettes

Preparation time: 20 minutes

Cooking time: 1 hour

Servings: 1

Ingredients:

- 1 1/2 cups pineapple chunks
- 1 sliced large onion
- 2 pounds thick steak
- 1 sliced medium bell pepper
- 1 bay leaf
- 1/4 cup vegetable oil
- 1/2 cup lemon juice
- 2 crushed garlic cloves

Directions:

1. Cut beef cubes and place in a plastic bag
2. Combine marinade ingredients in small bowl
3. Mix and pour over beef cubes
4. Seal the bag then refrigerate for 3 to 5 hours
5. Divide ingredients onion, beef cube, green pepper, pineapple
6. Grill about 9 minutes each side

Per serving: Calories: 304kcal; Fat: 0.53oz; Carbs: 0.39oz; Protein: 1.23oz; Sodium: 70mg; Potassium: 0.0102oz; Phosphorus: 0.0058oz

127. Open-Faced Beef Stir-Up

Preparation time: 10 minutes

Cooking time: 10 minutes

Servings: 6

Ingredients:

- 1/2 pound 95% lean ground beef
- 1/2 cup chopped sweet onion
- 1/2 cup shredded cabbage
- 1/4 cup herb pesto
- 6 hamburger buns, bottom halves only

Directions:

1. Sauté the beef and onion for 6 minutes or until beef is cooked.
2. Add the cabbage and sauté for 3 minutes more.
3. Stir in pesto and heat for 1 minute.
4. Divide the beef mixture into 6 portions and serve each on the bottom half of a hamburger bun, open-face.

Per serving: Calories: 120kcal; Fat: 0.11oz; Carbs: 0.18oz; Protein: 0.39oz; Sodium: 134mg; Potassium: 0.0070oz; Phosphorus: 0.0037oz

128. Roast Beef

Preparation time: 25 minutes

Cooking time: 55 minutes

Servings: 3

Ingredients:

- Quality rump or sirloin tip roast
- Pepper & herbs

Directions:

1. Place in a roasting pan on a shallow rack. Season with pepper and herbs. Insert meat thermometer in the center or thickest part of the roast.
2. Roast to the desired degree of doneness. After removing from over for about 15 minutes, let it chill. In the end, the roast should be moister than well done.

Per serving: Calories: 158kcal; Fat: 0.21oz; Carbs: 0oz; Protein: 0.85oz; Sodium: 55mg; Potassium: 0.0080oz; Phosphorus: 0.0073oz

129. Grilled Pork Tenderloin

Preparation time: 10 minutes

Cooking time: 20 minutes

Servings: 4

Ingredients:

- 1 lb pork tenderloin
- Low-sodium marinade of your choice (e.g., teriyaki, lemon-herb)
- Olive oil
- Salt and pepper, to taste

Directions:

1. Preheat the grill to medium-high heat.

2. Take any extra fat from the pork tenderloin by trimming it.
3. Marinate the pork tenderloin in your preferred low-sodium marinade for at least 30 mins or as directed.
4. To avoid food sticking, apply a coat of olive oil on the grill grates.
5. Take the pork tenderloin from the marinade, allowing any excess marinade to drip off.
6. Season with salt and pepper.
7. Grill the pork tenderloin for about 15-20 minutes, turning occasionally, 'til the internal temperature reaches 145 deg. F.
8. Remove from the grill then let it rest for a few minutes before slicing.
9. Slice the tenderloin into medallions and serve.

Per serving: Calories: 220kcal; Fat: 0.28oz; Carbs: 0oz; Protein: 1.23oz; Sodium: 120mg; Potassium: 0.0099oz; Phosphorus: 0.0053oz

130. Beef Stir-Fry

Preparation time: 15 minutes

Cooking time: 15 minutes

Servings: 4

Ingredients:

- 1 lb lean beef, thinly sliced
- Low-sodium soy sauce
- Ginger, grated
- Garlic, minced
- Broccoli florets
- Bell peppers, sliced
- Carrots, sliced
- Onion, sliced
- Olive oil
- Salt and pepper, to taste

Directions:

1. In a bowl, marinate the sliced beef with soy sauce, grated ginger, and minced garlic for 10 minutes.
2. Heat olive oil in a skillet/wok over medium-high heat.
3. Add the marinated beef and stir-fry for a few minutes until browned.
4. Add the vegetables (broccoli, bell peppers, carrots, and onion) and continue to stir-fry until the vegetables are tender-crisp.

5. Season with salt and pepper to taste.
6. Serve hot with steamed rice or quinoa.

Per serving: Calories: 300kcal; Fat: 0.35oz; Carbs: 0.35oz; Protein: 1.41oz; Sodium: 150mg; Potassium: 0.0106oz; Phosphorus: 0.0071oz

Chapter 7. Seafood Main Courses

131. Broiled Shrimp

Preparation time: 2 minutes

Cooking time: 5 minutes

Servings: 8

Ingredients:

- 1 lb. shrimp in shell
- 1/2 cup oil, melted
- 2 teaspoons lemon juice
- 2 tablespoons chopped onion
- 1 clove garlic, minced
- 1/8 teaspoon pepper

Directions:

1. Toss the shrimp with the oil, lemon juice, onion, garlic, and pepper in a bowl.
2. Spread the seasoned shrimp in a baking tray.
3. Broil for 5 minutes in an oven on broiler setting.
4. Serve warm.

Per serving: Calories: 164kcal; Fat: 0.46oz; Carbs: 0.035oz; Protein: 0.53oz; Sodium: 242mg; Potassium: 0.0080oz; Phosphorus: 0.0076oz

132. Poached Halibut In Mango Sauce

Preparation time: 10 minutes

Cooking time: 10 minutes

Servings: 4

Ingredients:

- 1-pound halibut
- 1/3 cup oil
- 1 rosemary sprig
- ½ teaspoon ground black pepper
- 1 teaspoon salt
- 1 teaspoon honey
- ¼ cup of mango juice
- 1 teaspoon cornstarch

Directions:

1. Put oil in the saucepan and melt it. Add rosemary sprig. Sprinkle the halibut with salt and ground black pepper. Put the fish in the boiling oil and poach it for 4 minutes.
2. Meanwhile, pour mango juice into the skillet. Add honey and bring the liquid to boil. Add cornstarch and whisk until the liquid starts to be thick. Then remove it from the heat.
3. Transfer the poached halibut to the plate and cut it on 4. Place every fish serving in the serving plate and top with mango sauce.

Per serving: Calories: 349kcal; Fat: 1.02oz; Carbs: 0.11oz; Protein: 0.63oz; Sodium: 29mg; Potassium: 0.0102oz; Phosphorus: 0.0054oz

133. Grilled Lemony Cod

Preparation time: 3 minutes

Cooking time: 10 minutes **Servings:** 4

Ingredients:

- 1 lb. cod fillets
- 1 teaspoon salt-free lemon pepper seasoning
- 1/4 cup lemon juice

Directions:

1. Rub the cod fillets with lemon pepper seasoning and lemon juice.
2. Grease a baking tray with cooking spray then place the salmon in the baking tray.
3. Bake the fish for 10 minutes at 350 deg. F in a preheated oven.
4. Serve warm.

Per serving: Calories: 155kcal; Fat: 0.25oz; Carbs: 0.035oz; Protein: 0.78oz; Sodium: 53mg; Potassium: 0.0092oz; Phosphorus: 0.0084oz

134. Haddock and Oiled Leeks

Preparation time: 5 minutes

Cooking time: 15 minutes

Servings: 2

Ingredients:

- 1 tbsp. oil
- 1 sliced leek
- ¼ tsp. black pepper

- 2 tsp. Chopped parsley
- 6 oz. haddock fillets
- ½ juiced lemon.

Directions:

1. Preheat the oven to 375 deg. F/Gas Mark 5.
2. Add the haddock fillets to baking or parchment paper and sprinkle with the black pepper.
3. Squeeze over the lemon juice and wrap into a parcel.
4. Bake the parcel on a baking tray for 10-15 minutes or until the fish is thoroughly cooked through.
5. Meanwhile, heat the oil in a medium-low heat in a small pan.
6. Add the leeks and parsley and sauté for 5-7 minutes until soft.
7. Serve the haddock fillets on a bed of oiled leeks and enjoy!

Per serving: Calories: 124kcal; Fat: 0.25oz; Carbs: 0oz; Protein: 0.53oz; Sodium: 161mg; Potassium: 0.0089oz; Phosphorus: 0.0078oz

135. Saucy Fish Dill

Preparation time: 5 minutes

Cooking time: 15 minutes

Servings: 4

Ingredients:

- 4 (4 oz.) salmon fillets

Dill Sauce:

- 1 cup whipped cream
- 4 minced garlic cloves
- ½ small onion, diced
- 3 tablespoons fresh or dried dill (as desired)
- ½ teaspoon ground pepper
- 1 teaspoon Mrs. Dash (optional)
- 2 drops of hot sauce (optional)

Directions:

1. Place the salmon fillets in a moderately shallow baking stray.
2. Whisk the cream and all the dill-sauce ingredients in a bowl.
3. Spread the dill-sauce over the fillets liberally.
4. Cover the fillet pan with a foil sheet then bake for 15 minutes at 350 deg. F.
5. Serve warm.

Per serving: Calories: 432kcal; Fat: 0.95oz; Carbs: 0.18oz; Protein: 1.27oz; Sodium: 180mg; Potassium: 0.0102oz; Phosphorus: 0.0058oz

136. Sardine Fish Cakes

Preparation time: 10 minutes

Cooking time: 10 minutes

Servings: 4

Ingredients:

- 11 oz. sardines, canned, drained
- 1/3 cup shallot, chopped
- 1 teaspoon chili flakes
- ½ teaspoon salt
- 2 tablespoon wheat flour, whole grain
- 1 egg, beaten
- 1 tablespoon chives, chopped
- 1 teaspoon olive oil
- 1 teaspoon oil

Directions:

1. Put the oil in your skillet and dissolve it. Add shallot and cook it until translucent. After this, transfer the shallot to the mixing bowl.
2. Add sardines, chili flakes, salt, flour, egg, chives, and mix up until smooth with the fork's help. Make the medium size cakes and place them in the skillet. Add olive oil.
3. Roast the fish cakes for 3 minutes from each side over medium heat. Dry the cooked fish cakes with a paper towel if needed and transfer to the serving plates.

Per serving: Calories: 221kcal; Fat: 0.42oz; Carbs: 0.18oz; Protein: 0.74oz; Sodium: 253mg; Potassium: 0.0056oz; Phosphorus: 0.0066oz

137. Oven-Fried Southern Style Catfish

Preparation time: 10 minutes

Cooking time: 35 minutes

Servings: 4

Ingredients:

- 1 egg white
- ½ cup of all-purpose flour
- ¼ cup of cornmeal
- ¼ cup of panko bread crumbs
- 1 teaspoon of salt-free Cajun seasoning

- 1 pound of catfish fillets

Directions:

1. Heat oven to 450 deg. F
2. Use cooking spray to spray a non-stick baking sheet
3. Using a bowl, beat the egg white until very soft peaks are formed. Don't over-beat
4. Use a sheet of wax paper and place the flour over it
5. Using a different sheet of wax paper to combine and mix the cornmeal, panko and the Cajun seasoning
6. Cut the catfish fillet into four pieces, then dip the fish in the flour, shaking off the excess
7. Dip coated fish in the egg white, rolling into the cornmeal mixture
8. Place the fish on the baking pan. Repeat with the remaining fish fillets
9. Use cooking spray to spray over the fish fillets. Bake for about 10 to 12 minutes or until the sides of the fillets become browned and crisp

Per serving: Calories: 250kcal; Fat: 0.35oz; Carbs: 0.67oz; Protein: 0.78oz; Sodium: 124mg; Potassium: 0.0071oz; Phosphorus: 0.0057oz

138. Herbed Vegetable Trout

Preparation time: 3 minutes

Cooking time: 12 minutes

Servings: 4

Ingredients:

- 14 oz. trout fillets
- 1/2 teaspoon herb seasoning blend
- 1 lemon, sliced
- 2 green onions, sliced
- 1 stalk celery, chopped
- 1 medium carrot, julienne

Directions:

1. Prepare and preheat a charcoal grill over moderate heat.
2. Place the trout fillets over a large piece of foil and drizzle herb seasoning on top.
3. Spread the lemon slices, carrots, celery, and green onions over the fish.
4. Cover the fish with foil and pack it.

5. Place the packed fish in the grill and cook for 15 minutes.
6. Once done, remove the foil from the fish.
7. Serve.

Per serving: Calories: 202kcal; Fat: 0.32oz; Carbs: 0.14oz; Protein: 0.63oz; Sodium: 82mg; Potassium: 0.0092oz; Phosphorus: 0.0066oz

139. Broiled Salmon Fillets

Preparation time: 5 minutes

Cooking time: 10 minutes

Servings: 4

Ingredients:

- 1 tablespoon ginger root, grated
- 1 clove garlic, minced
- ¼ cup maple syrup
- 1 tablespoon hot pepper sauce
- 4 salmon fillets, skinless

Directions:

1. Grease a pan with cooking spray and place it over moderate heat.
2. Add the ginger and garlic and sauté for 3 minutes then transfer to a bowl.
3. Add the hot pepper sauce and maple syrup to the ginger-garlic.
4. Mix well and keep this mixture aside.
5. Place the salmon fillet in a suitable baking tray, greased with cooking oil.
6. Brush the maple sauce over the fillets liberally
7. Broil them for 10 minutes in the oven at broiler settings.
8. Serve warm.

Per serving: Calories: 289kcal; Fat: 0.39oz; Carbs: 0.46oz; Protein: 1.20oz; Sodium: 80mg; Potassium: 0.0082oz; Phosphorus: 0.0081oz

140. Spiced Honey Salmon

Preparation time: 3 minutes

Cooking time: 15 minutes

Servings: 4

Ingredients:

- 3 tablespoons honey
- 3/4 teaspoon lemon peel

- 1/2 teaspoon black pepper
- 1/2 teaspoon garlic powder
- 1 teaspoon water
- 16 oz. salmon fillets
- 2 tablespoons olive oil
- Dill, chopped, to serve

Directions:

1. Whisk the lemon peel with honey, garlic powder, hot water, and ground pepper in a small bowl.
2. Rub this honey mixture over the salmon fillet liberally.
3. Set a suitable skillet over moderate heat and add olive oil to heat.
4. Set the spiced salmon fillets in the pan and sear them for 4 minutes per side.
5. Garnish with dill.
6. Serve warm.

Per serving: Calories: 264kcal; Fat: 0.49oz; Carbs: 0.49oz; Protein: 0.81oz; Sodium: 55mg; Potassium: 0.0108oz; Phosphorus: 0.0061oz

141. Fish Tacos

Preparation time: 10 minutes

Cooking time: 35 minutes

Servings: 6

Ingredients:

- 1½ cup of cabbage
- ½ cup of red onion
- ½ bunch of cilantros
- 1 garlic clove
- 2 limes
- 1 pound of cod fillets
- ½ teaspoon of ground cumin
- ½ teaspoon of chili powder
- ¼ teaspoon of black pepper
- 1 tablespoon of olive oil
- ½ cup of mayonnaise
- ¼ cup of sour cream
- 2 tablespoons of almond milk
- 12 (6-inch) corn tortillas

Directions:

1. Shred the cabbage, chop the onion & cilantro, and mince the garlic. Set aside

2. Use a dish to place in the fish fillets, then squeeze half a lime juice over the fish. Sprinkle the fish fillets with the minced garlic, cumin, black pepper, chili powder, and olive oil. Turn the fish filets to coat with the marinade, then refrigerate for about 15 to 30 minutes
3. Prepare salsa Blanca by mixing the mayonnaise, almond milk, sour cream, and the other half of the lime juice. Stir to combine, then place in the refrigerator to chill
4. Broil in oven, and cover the broiler pan with aluminum foil. Broil the coated fish fillets for about 10 minutes or until the flesh becomes opaque and white and flakes easily. Remove from the oven, slightly cool, and then flake the fish into bigger pieces
5. Heat the corn tortillas in a pan, one at a time until it becomes soft and warm, then wrap in a dish towel to keep them warm
6. To assemble the tacos, place a piece of the fish on the tortilla, topping with the salsa Blanca, cabbage, cilantro, red onion, and the lime wedges.
7. Serve with hot sauce if you desire

Per serving: Calories: 363kcal; Fat: 0.67oz; Carbs: 1.06oz; Protein: 0.63oz; Sodium: 194mg; Potassium: 0.0073oz; Phosphorus: 0.0115oz

142. Salmon Baked in Foil with Fresh Thyme

Preparation time: 10 minutes

Cooking time: 30 minutes

Servings: 4

Ingredients:

- 4 fresh thyme sprigs
- 4 garlic cloves, peeled, roughly chopped
- 16 oz. salmon fillets (4 oz. each fillet)
- ½ teaspoon salt
- ½ teaspoon ground black pepper
- 4 tablespoons cream
- 4 teaspoons butter
- ¼ teaspoon cumin seeds

Directions:

1. Line the baking tray with foil. Sprinkle the fish fillets with salt, ground black pepper, cumin seeds, and arrange them in the tray with oil.
2. Add thyme sprig on the top of every fillet. Then

add cream, butter, and garlic. Bake the fish for 30 minutes at 345 deg. F. Serve.

Per serving: Calories: 198kcal; Fat: 0.41oz; Carbs: 0.063oz; Protein: 0.79oz; Sodium: 166mg; Potassium: 0.0092oz; Phosphorus: 0.0079oz

143. Shrimp in Garlic Sauce

Preparation time: 10 minutes

Cooking time: 6 minutes

Servings: 4

Ingredients:

- 3 tablespoons butter (unsalted)
- 1/4 cup onion, minced
- 3 cloves garlic, minced
- 1-pound shrimp, shelled and deveined
- 1/2 cup half and half creamer
- 1/4 cup white wine
- 2 tablespoons fresh basil
- Black pepper to taste

Directions:

1. Add butter to a pan in a medium low heat.
2. Let it melt.
3. Add the onion and garlic.
4. Cook for it 1-2 minutes.
5. Add the shrimp then cook for 2 minutes.
6. Transfer shrimp on a serving platter and set aside.
7. Add the rest of the ingredients.
8. Simmer for 3 minutes.
9. Pour sauce over the shrimp and serve.

Per serving: Calories: 482kcal; Fat: 0.39oz; Carbs: 1.62oz; Protein: 1.16oz; Sodium: 213mg; Potassium: 0.0111oz; Phosphorus: 0.0105oz

144. Steamed Fish with Garlic

Preparation time: 15min

Cooking time: 45 minutes

Servings: 4

Ingredients:

- 2 (6 ounce) fillets cod fillets
- 3 tablespoons olive oil
- 1 onion, chopped
- 4 cloves garlic, minced
- 3 pinches dried rosemary
- Ground black pepper to taste
- 1 lemon, halved

Directions:

1. Preheat oven to 350 deg. F.
2. Place cod fillets on an 18x18-inch piece of aluminum foil; top with oil. Sprinkle onion, garlic, rosemary, and pepper over oil and cod. Squeeze juice from ½ lemon evenly on top.
3. Lift up bottom then top ends of the aluminum foil towards the center; fold together to 1" above the cod. Flatten short ends of the aluminum foil; fold over to within 1" of the sides of the cod. Place foil package on a baking sheet.
4. Bake in the preheated oven 'til haddock flakes easily with a fish, about 45 minutes. Let sit, about 5 minutes. Open ends of the packet carefully; squeeze juice from the remaining 1/2 lemon on top.

Per serving: Calories: 171kcal; Fat: 0.40oz; Carbs: 0.18oz; Protein: 0.50oz; Sodium: 208mg; Potassium: 0.0027oz; Phosphorus: 0.0024oz

145. Citrus Glazed Salmon

Preparation time: 5 minutes

Cooking time: 12 minutes

Servings: 4

Ingredients:

- 2 garlic cloves, crushed
- 1 1/2 tablespoons lemon juice
- 2 tablespoons olive oil
- 1 tablespoon oil
- 1 tablespoon Dijon mustard
- 2 dashes cayenne pepper
- 1 teaspoon dried basil leaves
- 1 teaspoon dried dill
- 24 oz. salmon filet

Directions:

1. Place a 1-quart saucepan over moderate heat and add the oil, garlic, lemon juice, mustard, cayenne pepper, dill, and basil to the pan.
2. Stir this mixture for 5 minutes after it has boiled.
3. Prepare and preheat a charcoal grill over moderate heat.

4. Place the fish on a foil sheet then fold the edges to make a foil tray.

5. Pour the prepared sauce over the fish.

6. Place the fish in the foil in the preheated grill and cook for 12 minutes.

7. Slice and serve.

Per serving: Calories: 401kcal; Fat: 0.74oz; Carbs: 0.035oz; Protein: 1.73oz; Sodium: 256mg; Potassium: 0.0122oz; Phosphorus: 0.0075oz

146. Cilantro-Lime Cod

Preparation time: 10 minutes

Cooking time: 35 minutes

Servings: 4

Ingredients:

- ½ cup of mayonnaise
- ½ cup of fresh chopped cilantro
- 2 tablespoon of lime juice
- 1 pound of cod fillets

Directions:

1. Combine and mix the mayonnaise, cilantro, and lime juice in a medium bowl, remove ¼ cup to another bowl and put aside. To be served as fish sauce

2. Spread the remaining mayonnaise mixture over the cod fillets

3. Use cooking spray to spray a large skillet, then heat over medium-high heat

4. Place in the cod fillets, and cook for about 8 minutes or until the fish becomes firm and moist, turning just once

5. Serve with the ¼ cilantro-lime sauce

Per serving: Calories: 292kcal; Fat: 0.81oz; Carbs: 0.035oz; Protein: 0.71oz; Sodium: 228mg; Potassium: 0.0084oz; Phosphorus: 0.0045oz

147. Baked Fennel and Garlic Sea Bass

Preparation time: 5 minutes

Cooking time: 15 minutes

Servings: 2 servings

Ingredients:

- 1 lemon
- ½ sliced fennel bulb
- 6 oz. sea bass fillets
- 1 teaspoon black pepper
- 2 garlic cloves
- 1 salmon filet

Directions:

1. Preheat the oven to 375 deg. F/Gas Mark 5.

2. Sprinkle black pepper over the Sea Bass.

3. Slice the fennel bulb and garlic cloves.

4. Add 1 salmon fillet and half the fennel and garlic to one sheet of baking paper or tin foil.

5. Squeeze in 1/2 lemon juices.

6. Repeat for the other fillet.

7. Fold and add to the oven for 12-15 minutes or until fish is thoroughly cooked through.

8. Meanwhile, add boiling water to your couscous, cover, and allow to steam.

9. Serve with your choice of rice or salad.

Per serving: Calories: 221kcal; Fat: 0.071oz; Carbs: 0.11oz; Protein: 0.49oz; Sodium: 119mg; Potassium: 0.0105oz; Phosphorus: 0.0053oz

148. Oregon Tuna Patties

Preparation time: 10 minutes

Cooking time: 15 minutes

Servings: 4

Ingredients:

- 1 (14.75 ounce) can tuna
- 2 tablespoons butter
- 1 medium onion, chopped
- 2/3 cup graham cracker crumbs
- 2 egg whites, beaten
- 1/4 cup chopped fresh parsley
- 1 teaspoon dry mustard
- 3 tablespoons olive oil

Directions:

1. Drain the tuna, reserving 3/4 cup of the liquid. Flake the meat. Melt butter in a huge skillet over medium- high heat. Add onion then cook until tender.

2. In your medium bowl, combine the onions with the reserved tuna liquid, 1/3 of the graham cracker crumbs, egg whites, parsley, mustard and tuna. Mix 'til well blended, then shape into six patties. Coat patties in remaining cracker crumbs.

3. Heat olive in a huge skillet in a medium heat. Cook

patties 'til browned, then carefully turn and brown on the other side.

Per serving: Calories: 204kcal; Fat: 0.54oz; Carbs: 0.23oz; Protein: 0.37oz; Sodium: 111mg; Potassium: 0.0058oz; Phosphorus: 0.0037oz

149. Fish with Mushrooms

Preparation time: 5 minutes

Cooking time: 16 minutes

Servings: 4

Ingredients:

- 1-pound cod fillet
- 2 tablespoons butter
- ¼ cup white onion, chopped
- 1 cup fresh mushrooms
- 1 teaspoon dried thyme

Directions:

1. Put the fish in a baking pan.
2. Preheat your oven to 450 deg. F.
3. Melt the butter and cook onion and mushroom for 1 minute.
4. Spread mushroom mixture on top of the fish.
5. Season with thyme.
6. Bake in the oven for 15 minutes.

Per serving: Calories: 156kcal; Fat: 0.25oz; Carbs: 0.11oz; Protein: 0.74oz; Sodium: 110mg; Potassium: 0.0127oz; Phosphorus: 0.0079oz

150. Chili Mussels

Preparation time: 7 minutes

Cooking time: 10 minutes

Servings: 4

Ingredients:

- 1-pound mussels
- 1 chili pepper, chopped
- 1 cup chicken stock
- ½ cup almond milk
- 1 teaspoon olive oil
- 1 teaspoon minced garlic
- 1 teaspoon ground coriander
- ½ teaspoon salt
- 1 cup fresh parsley, chopped
- 4 tablespoons lemon juice

Directions:

1. Pour almond milk into the saucepan. Add chili pepper, chicken stock, olive oil, minced garlic, ground coriander, salt, and lemon juice.
2. Bring the liquid to boil and add mussels. Boil the mussel for 4 minutes or until they will open shells. Then add chopped parsley and mix up the meal well. Remove it from the heat.

Per serving: Calories: 136kcal; Fat: 0.17oz; Carbs: 0.26oz; Protein: 0.54oz; Sodium: 219.6mg; Potassium: 0.011oz; Phosphorus: 0.0064oz

Chapter 8.   Sides and Salad

151. Grapes Jicama Salad

Preparation time: 5 minutes

Cooking time: 0 minutes

Servings: 2

Ingredients:

- 1 jicama, peeled and sliced
- 1 carrot, sliced
- 1/2 medium red onion, sliced
- 1 ¼ cup seedless grapes
- 1/3 cup fresh basil leaves
- 1 tablespoon apple cider vinegar
- 1 ½ tablespoon lemon juice
- 1 ½ tablespoon lime juice

Directions:

1. Put all the salad ingredients into a suitable salad bowl.
2. Toss them well and refrigerate for 1 hour.
3. Serve.

Per serving: Calories: 203kcal; Fat: 0.035oz; Carbs: 0.88oz; Protein: 0.14oz; Sodium: 44mg; Potassium: 0.0116oz; Phosphorus: 0.0050oz

152. Couscous Salad

Preparation time: 5 minutes

Cooking time: 5 minutes

Servings: 5 servings

Ingredients:

- 3 cups of water
- 1/2 tsp. cinnamon tea
- 1/2 tsp. cumin tea
- 1 tsp. honey soup
- 2 tbsp. lemon juice
- 3 cups quick-cooking couscous
- 2 tbsp. tea of olive oil
- 1 green onion,
- Finely chopped 1 small carrot, finely diced
- 1/2 red pepper,
- Finely diced fresh coriander

Directions:

1. Stir in the water with the cinnamon, cumin, honey, and lemon juice then bring to a boil. Put the couscous in it, cover it, and remove it from the heat.
2. To swell the couscous, stir with a fork. Add the vegetables, fresh herbs, and olive oil. It is possible to serve the salad warm or cold.

Per serving: Calories: 190kcal; Fat: 0.035oz; Carbs: 1.34oz; Protein: 0.21oz; Sodium: 4mg; Potassium: 0.0041oz; Phosphorus: 0.0029oz

153. Carrot Jicama Salad

Preparation time: 5 minutes

Cooking time: 0 minutes

Servings: 2

Ingredients:

- 2 cup carrots, julienned
- 1 1/2 cups jicama, julienned
- 2 tablespoons lime juice
- 1 tablespoon olive oil
- ½ tablespoon apple cider
- ½ teaspoon brown Swerve

Directions:

1. Put all the salad ingredients into a suitable salad bowl.
2. Toss them well and refrigerate for 1 hour.
3. Serve.

Per serving: Calories: 173kcal; Fat: 0.25oz; Carbs: 1.09oz; Protein: 0.071oz; Sodium: 80mg; Potassium: 0.0106oz; Phosphorus: 0.0034oz

154. Italian Cucumber Salad

Preparation time: 5 minutes

Cooking time: 0 minutes

Servings: 2

Ingredients:

- 1/4 cup rice vinegar
- 1/8 teaspoon stevia

- 1/2 teaspoon olive oil
- 1/8 teaspoon black pepper
- 1/2 cucumber, sliced
- 1 cup carrots, sliced
- 2 tablespoons green onion, sliced
- 2 tablespoons red bell pepper, sliced
- 1/2 teaspoon Italian seasoning blend

Directions:

1. Put all the salad ingredients into a suitable salad bowl.
2. Toss them well and refrigerate for 1 hour.
3. Serve.

Per serving: Calories: 112kcal; Fat: 2g; Carbs: 23g; Protein: 3g; Sodium: 43mg; Potassium: 329mg; Phosphorus: 198mg

155. Panzanella Salad

Preparation time: 10 minutes
Cooking time: 5 minutes
Servings: 4
Ingredients:

- 2 cucumbers, chopped
- 1 red onion, sliced
- 2 red bell peppers, chopped
- ¼ cup fresh cilantro, chopped
- 1 tablespoon capers
- 1 oz whole-grain bread, chopped
- 1 tablespoon canola oil
- ½ teaspoon minced garlic
- 1 tablespoon Dijon mustard
- 1 teaspoon olive oil
- 1 teaspoon lime juice

Directions:

1. Pour canola oil into the skillet then bring it to boil.
2. Add chopped bread and roast it until crunchy (3-5 minutes).
3. Meanwhile, in the salad bowl, combine sliced red onion, cucumbers, bell peppers, cilantro, capers, and mix up gently.
4. Make the dressing: mix up together lime juice, olive oil, Dijon mustard, and minced garlic.
5. Put the dressing over the salad and stir it directly before serving.

Per serving: Calories: 224kcal; Fat: 0.35oz; Carbs: 0.92oz; Protein: 0.25oz; Sodium: 201mg; Potassium: 0.0115oz; Phosphorus: 0.0030oz

156. Squash and Cranberries

Preparation time: 10 minutes
Cooking time: 30 minutes
Servings: 2
Ingredients:

- 1 tablespoon coconut oil
- 1 butternut squash, peeled and cubed
- 2 garlic cloves, minced
- 1 small yellow onion, chopped
- 12 ounces coconut almond milk
- 1 teaspoon curry powder
- 1 teaspoon cinnamon powder
- ½ cup cranberries

Directions:

1. Spread squash pieces on a lined baking sheet, place in the oven at 425 deg. F, bake for 15 minutes and leave to one side.
2. Heat up a pan with the oil over medium high heat, add garlic and onion, stir and cook for 5 minutes.
3. Add roasted squash, stir and cook for 3 minutes.
4. Add coconut almond milk, cranberries, cinnamon and curry powder, stir and cook for 5 minutes more.
5. Divide between plates and serve as a side dish!
6. Enjoy!

Per serving: Calories: 518kcal; Fat: 1.68oz; Carbs: 0.88oz; Protein: 0.19oz; Sodium: 75mg; Potassium: 0.0041oz; Phosphorus: 0.0039oz

157. Butterscotch Apple Salad

Preparation time: 5 minutes
Cooking time: 0 minutes
Servings: 6
Ingredients:

- 3 cups jazz apples, chopped
- 8 oz. canned crushed pineapple
- 8 oz. whipped topping
- 1/2 cup butterscotch topping
- 1/3 cup almonds

- 1/4 cup butterscotch

Directions:

1. Put all the salad ingredients into a suitable salad bowl.
2. Toss them well and refrigerate for 1 hour.
3. Serve.

Per serving: Calories: 293kcal; Fat: 0.46oz; Carbs: 0.63oz; Protein: 0.14oz; Sodium: 52mg; Potassium: 0.0104oz; Phosphorus: 0.0071oz

158. Cool Cucumber Salad

Preparation time: 25 minutes

Cooking time: 10 minutes

Servings: 6

Ingredients:

- 2 cups of 1/4"-thick sliced cucumbers, fresh, peeled or unpeeled
- 2 tbsp. of salad dressing, Caesar or Italian, no sodium
- Pepper, ground, as desired

Directions:

1. In medium bowl with secure lid, combine sliced cucumbers with salad dressing.
2. Cover the bowl with the lid, then shake, coating cucumbers.
3. Sprinkle using pepper. Place in refrigerator. Serve chilled.

Per serving: Calories: 26kcal; Fat: 0.053oz; Carbs: 0.071oz; Protein: 0oz; Sodium: 0mg; Potassium: 0.0031oz; Phosphorus: 0.0004oz

159. Fruity Zucchini Salad

Preparation time: 5 minutes

Cooking time: 5 minutes

Servings: 4 servings

Ingredients:

- 400g zucchini
- 1 small onion
- 4 tbsp. olive oil
- 100g pineapple preserve, drained
- Salt, paprika
- thyme

Directions:

1. Dice the onions and sauté in the oil until translucent.
2. Cut the zucchini into slices and add. Season with salt, paprika, and thyme.
3. Let cool and mix with the cut pineapple.

Per serving: Calories: 150kcal; Fat: 0.35oz; Carbs: 0.35oz; Protein: 0.071oz; Sodium: 28mg; Potassium: 0.0078oz; Phosphorus: 0.0008oz

160. Garlicky Penne Pasta with Asparagus

Preparation time: 10 minutes

Cooking time: 10 minutes

Servings: 4

Ingredients:

- 2 tbsp. butter
- 1 lb. asparagus, cut into 2-inch pieces
- 2 tsp lemon juice
- 4 cup whole wheat penne pasta, cooked
- ¼ cup shredded parmesan cheese
- ¼ tsp tabasco® hot sauce

Directions:

1. Add olive oil and butter in a skillet over medium heat.
2. Fry garlic & red pepper flakes for 2-3 minutes.
3. Add asparagus, Tabasco sauce, lemon juice, and black pepper to skillet and cook for a further 6 minutes.
4. Add hot pasta and cheese. Toss and serve.

Per serving: Calories: 387kcal; Fat: 0oz; Carbs: 1.73oz; Protein: 0.46oz; Sodium: 93mg; Potassium: 0.0091oz; Phosphorus: 0.0089oz

161. Roasted Root Vegetables

Preparation time: 10 minutes

Cooking time: 25 minutes

Servings: 6

Ingredients:

- 1 cup chopped turnips
- 1 cup chopped rutabaga
- 1 cup chopped parsnips
- 1 tablespoon extra-virgin olive oil
- 1 teaspoon fresh chopped rosemary
- Freshly ground black pepper

Directions:

1. Preheat the oven to 420 deg. F.
2. Toss the turnips, rutabaga, and parsnips with the olive oil and rosemary.
3. Assemble in a single layer on a baking sheet, and season with pepper.
4. Roast until the vegetables are tender then browned, 20 to 25 minutes, stirring once.

Per serving: Calories: 52kcal; Fat: 0.071oz; Carbs: 0.25oz; Protein: 0.035oz; Sodium: 22mg; Potassium: 0.0072oz; Phosphorus: 0.0012oz

162. Cauliflower and Leeks

Preparation time: 10 minutes

Cooking time: 20 minutes

Servings: 4

Ingredients:

- 1 and ½ cups leeks, chopped
- 1 and ½ cups cauliflower florets
- 2 garlic cloves, minced
- 1 and ½ cups artichoke hearts
- 2 tablespoons coconut oil, melted
- Black pepper to taste

Directions:

1. Heat up a pan with the oil over medium-high heat, add garlic, leeks, cauliflower florets and artichoke hearts, stir and cook for 20 minutes.
2. Add black pepper, stir, divide between plates and serve.
3. Enjoy!

Per serving: Calories: 192kcal; Fat: 0.24oz; Carbs: 1.24oz; Protein: 0.18oz; Sodium: 75mg; Potassium: 0.0041oz; Phosphorus: 0.0039oz

163. Cucumber Couscous Salad

Preparation time: 5 minutes

Cooking time: 0 minutes

Servings: 4

Ingredients:

- 1 cucumber, sliced
- ½ cup red bell pepper, sliced
- ¼ cup sweet onion, sliced
- ¼ cup parsley, chopped

- ½ cup couscous, cooked
- 2 tablespoons olive oil
- 2 tablespoons rice vinegar
- 2 tablespoons feta cheese crumbled
- 1 ½ teaspoon dried basil
- 1/4 teaspoon black pepper

Directions:

1. Put all the salad ingredients into a suitable salad bowl.
2. Toss them well and refrigerate for 1 hour.
3. Serve.

Per serving: Calories: 202kcal; Fat: 0.35oz; Carbs: 1.13oz; Protein: 0.21oz; Sodium: 258mg; Potassium: 0.0074oz; Phosphorus: 0.0068oz

164. Feta Bean Salad

Preparation time: 5 minutes

Cooking time: 20 minutes

Servings: 2

Ingredients:

- 1 tbsp of olive oil
- 2 egg whites (boiled)
- 1 cup of green beans (8 oz)
- 1 tbsp of onion
- 1/2 red chili
- 1/8 cup of cilantro
- 1 1/2 tbsp lime juice
- 1/4 tbsp of black pepper

Directions:

1. Remove the ends off the green beans and cut them into small pieces.
2. Chop the onion, cilantro, and chili and mix it.
3. Use a steamer to cook green beans for 5- 10 minutes and rinse with cold water once done.
4. Place all the mixed dry ingredients together in two serving bowls.
5. Chop the egg whites up and place them on top of the salad with crumbled feta.
6. Drizzle a pinch of olive oil with black pepper on top.

Per serving: Calories: 255kcal; Fat: 0.85oz; Carbs: 0.28oz; Protein: 0.18oz; Sodium: 215.6mg; Potassium: 0.0074oz; Phosphorus: 0.0044oz

165. Minty Olives Salad

Preparation time: 10 minutes

Cooking time: 0 minutes

Servings: 4

Ingredients:

- 1 cup kalamata olives, pitted and sliced
- 1 cup black olives, pitted and halved
- 1 red onion, chopped
- 2 tablespoons oregano, chopped
- 1 tablespoon mint, chopped
- 2 tablespoons balsamic vinegar
- ¼ cup olive oil
- 2 teaspoons Italian herbs, dried
- a pinch of sea salt & black pepper

Directions:

1. In a salad bowl, mix the olives then the rest of the ingredients, toss then serve cold.

Per serving: Calories: 190kcal; Fat: 0.29oz; Carbs: 0.41oz; Protein: 0.16oz; Sodium: 75mg; Potassium: 0.0041oz; Phosphorus: 0.0039oz

166. Farmer's Salad

Preparation time: 5 minutes

Cooking time: 5 minutes

Servings: 2 servings

Ingredients:

- 4 tablespoons mixed leaf salads
- ¾ cup red pepper, diced
- 1 ½ green beans
- 4 tablespoons feta cheese
- 1 tbsp. wine vinegar
- 1 tbsp. diced onions
- Salt, pepper, sugar
- 2 tbsp. olive oil

Directions:

1. Mix vinegar with onions, oil, and spices and mix with the salad.
2. Cut the sheep's cheese into cubes and serve with the salad. It goes well with baguette or flatbread with herb butter.

Per serving: Calories: 187kcal; Fat: 0.56oz; Carbs: 0.14oz; Protein: 0.28oz; Sodium: 188mg; Potassium: 0.0104oz; Phosphorus: 0.0060oz

167. Mint Zucchini

Preparation time: 10 minutes

Cooking time: 7 minutes

Servings: 4

Ingredients:

- 2 tablespoons mint
- 2 zucchinis, halved lengthwise and then slice into half moons
- 1 tablespoon coconut oil, melted
- ½ tablespoon dill, chopped
- A pinch of cayenne pepper

Directions:

1. Heat up a pan with the oil in a medium-high heat, add zucchinis, stir and cook for 6 minutes.
2. Add cayenne, dill and mint, stir, cook for 1 minute more, divide between plates and serve.
3. Enjoy!

Per serving: Calories: 46kcal; Fat: 0.13oz; Carbs: 0.12oz; Protein: 0.046oz; Sodium: 75mg; Potassium: 0.0045oz; Phosphorus: 0.0042oz

168. Garlic Mashed Carrots

Preparation time: 5 minutes

Cooking time: 20 minutes

Servings: 4

Ingredients:

- 2 medium carrots, peeled and sliced
- ¼ cup butter
- ¼ cup 1% low-fat almond milk
- 2 garlic cloves

Directions:

4. Double-boil or soak the carrots to lower potassium if you are on a low potassium diet.
5. Boil carrots and garlic until soft. Drain.
6. Beat the carrots and garlic with butter and almond milk until smooth.

Per serving: Calories: 168kcal; Fat: 0oz; Carbs: 1.02oz; Protein: 0.18oz; Sodium: 59mg; Potassium: 0.0057oz; Phosphorus: 0.0020oz

169. Carrot-Apple Casserole

Preparation time: 15 minutes

Cooking time: 50 minutes

Servings: 8

Ingredients:

- 6 large carrots, peeled and sliced
- 4 large apples, peeled and sliced
- 3 tbsp. butter
- ½ cup apple juice
- 5 tbsp. all-purpose flour
- 2 tbsp. brown sugar
- ½ tsp ground nutmeg

Directions:

1. Preheat oven to 350 deg. F.
2. Let the carrots boil for 5 minutes or until tender. Drain.
3. Arrange the carrots and apples in a large casserole dish.
4. Mix the flour, brown sugar, and nutmeg in a small bowl.
5. Rub in butter to make a crumb topping.
6. Sprinkle the crumb over the carrots and apples, then drizzle with juice.
7. Bake until bubbling and golden brown.

Per serving: Calories: 245kcal; Fat: 0.21oz; Carbs: 1.73oz; Protein: 0.035oz; Sodium: 91mg; Potassium: 0.0060oz; Phosphorus: 0.0006oz

170. Cucumber Salad

Preparation time: 5 minutes

Cooking time: 5 minutes

Servings: 4

Ingredients:

- 1 tbsp. dried dill
- 1 onion
- ¼ cup water
- 1 cup vinegar
- 3 cucumbers
- ¾ cup white sugar

Directions:

1. In a bowl add all ingredients then mix well.
2. Serve with dressing.

Per serving: Calories: 49kcal; Fat: 0oz; Carbs: 0.39oz; Protein: 0.035oz; Sodium: 241mg; Potassium: 0.0060oz; Phosphorus: 0.0008oz

Chapter 9.   Snacks

171. Rosemary and White Bean Dip

Preparation time: 10 minutes

Cooking time: 10 minutes

Servings: 10 (¼ cup per serving)

Ingredients:

- 1 (15-ounce) can cannellini beans, rinsed & drained
- 2 tablespoons extra-virgin olive oil
- 1 garlic clove, peeled
- 1 teaspoon finely chopped fresh rosemary
- Pinch cayenne pepper
- Freshly ground black pepper
- 1 (7.5-ounce) jar marinated artichoke hearts, drained

Directions:

1. Blend the beans, oil, garlic, rosemary, cayenne pepper, and black pepper in a food processor 'til smooth.
2. Add the artichoke hearts, and pulse until roughly chopped but not puréed.

Per serving: Calories: 75kcal; Fat: 0.18oz; Carbs: 0.21oz; Protein: 0.071oz; Sodium: 139mg; Potassium: 0.0026oz; Phosphorus: 0.0045oz

172. Sautéed Spicy Cabbage

Preparation time: 15 minutes

Cooking time: 5 minutes

Servings: 6

Ingredients:

- 3 tablespoons olive oil
- 3 cups chopped green cabbage
- 3 cups chopped red cabbage
- 2 garlic cloves, minced
- 1/8 teaspoon cayenne pepper
- Pinch salt

Directions:

1. Cook olive oil in a large skillet over medium heat.
2. Stir in red and green cabbage and the garlic; sauté until the leaves wilt and are tender, about 4 to 5 minutes.

3. Sprinkle the vegetables with the cayenne pepper and salt, toss, and serve.

Per serving: Calories: 86kcal; Fat: 0.21oz; Carbs: 0.81oz; Protein: 0.035oz; Sodium: 46mg; Potassium: 0.0067oz; Phosphorus: 0.0010oz

173. Sweet And Spicy Tortilla Chips

Preparation time: 10 minutes

Cooking time: 8 minutes

Servings: 6

Ingredients:

- 1/4 cup butter
- 1 teaspoon brown sugar
- 1/2 teaspoon ground chili powder
- 1/2 teaspoon garlic powder
- 1/2 teaspoon ground cumin
- 1/4 teaspoon ground cayenne pepper
- 6 flour tortillas, 6" size

Directions:

1. Preheat oven to 425 deg. f.
2. Grease a baking sheet with cooking spray.
3. Add all spices, brown sugar, and melted butter to a small bowl.
4. Mix well and set this mixture aside.
5. Slice the tortillas into 8 wedges and brush them with the sugar mixture.
6. Spread them on the baking sheet then bake them for 8 minutes.
7. Serve fresh.

Per serving: Calories: 115kcal; Fat: 0.25oz; Carbs: 0.39oz; Protein: 0.071oz; Sodium: 156mg; Potassium: 0.0015oz; Phosphorus: 0.0016oz

174. Veggie Snack

Preparation time: 5 minutes

Cooking time: 10 minutes

Servings: 2

Ingredients:

- 2 large yellow pepper

- 10 carrots
- 10 stalks celery

Directions:

1. Clean the carrots and rinse them under running water.
2. Rinse celery and yellow pepper. Remove the seeds of pepper and chop the veggies into small sticks.
3. Put in a bowl and serve.

Per serving: Calories: 189kcal; Fat: 0.035oz; Carbs: 1.55oz; Protein: 0.18oz; Sodium: 282mg; Potassium: 0oz; Phosphorus: 0oz

175. Garlic Oyster Crackers

Preparation time: 10 minutes

Cooking time: 45 minutes

Servings: 4

Ingredients:

- 1/2 cup butter-flavored popcorn oil
- 1 tablespoon garlic powder
- 7 cups oyster crackers
- 2 teaspoon dried dill weed

Directions:

1. Preheat oven to 250 deg. F.
2. Mix garlic powder with oil in a large bowl.
3. Toss in crackers and mix well to coat evenly.
4. Sprinkle the dill weed over the crackers and toss well again.
5. Spread the crackers on the baking sheet and bake them for 45 minutes.
6. Toss them every 15 minutes.
7. Serve fresh.

Per serving: Calories: 118kcal; Fat: 0.25oz; Carbs: 0.42oz; Protein: 0.071oz; Sodium: 166mg; Potassium: 0.0007oz; Phosphorus: 0.0005oz

176. Addictive Pretzels

Preparation time: 10 minutes

Cooking time: 1 hour

Servings: 6

Ingredients:

- 32-ounce bag unsalted pretzels
- 1 cup canola oil
- 2 tablespoon seasoning mix

- 3 teaspoon garlic powder
- 3 teaspoon dried dill weed

Directions:

1. Preheat oven to 175 deg. f.
2. Place the pretzels on a cooking sheet and break them into pieces.
3. Mix garlic powder and dill in a bowl and reserve half of the mixture.
4. Mix the remaining half with seasoning mix and ¾ cup of canola oil.
5. Pour this oil over the pretzels and brush them liberally
6. Bake the pieces for 1 hour then flip them to bake for another 15 minutes.
7. Allow them to cool then sprinkle the remaining dill mixture and drizzle more oil on top.
8. Serve fresh and warm.

Per serving: Calories: 184kcal; Fat: 0.28oz; Carbs: 0.78oz; Protein: 0.071oz; Sodium: 60mg; Potassium: 0.0015oz; Phosphorus: 0.0010oz

177. Apple & Strawberry Snack

Preparation time: 5 minutes

Cooking time: 2 minutes

Servings: 1

Ingredients:

- ½ apple, cored and sliced
- 2-3 strawberries
- Dash of ground cinnamon
- 2-3 drops stevia 2-3 drops

Directions:

1. In a bowl, mix strawberries and apples and sprinkle with stevia and cinnamon.
2. Microwave for about 1-2 minutes. Serve warm.

Per serving: Calories: 145kcal; Fat: 0.028oz; Carbs: 1.21oz; Protein: 0.056oz; Sodium: 20mg; Potassium: 0oz; Phosphorus: 0oz

178. Sweet Savory Meatballs

Preparation time: 10 minutes

Cooking time: 20 minutes

Servings: 12

Ingredients:

- 1-pound ground turkey
- 1 large egg
- 1/4 cup bread crumbs
- 2 tablespoon onion, finely chopped
- 1 teaspoon garlic powder
- 1/2 teaspoon black pepper
- 1/4 cup canola oil
- 6-ounce grape jelly
- 1/4 cup chili sauce

Directions:

1. Place all ingredients except chili sauce and jelly in a large mixing bowl.
2. Mix well until evenly mixed then make small balls out of this mixture.
3. It will make about 48 meatballs. Spread them out on a greased pan on a stovetop.
4. Cook them over medium heat until brown on all the sides.
5. Mix chili sauce with jelly in a microwave-safe bowl then heat it for 2 minutes in the microwave.
6. Pour this chili sauce mixture onto the meatballs in the pan.
7. Transfer the meatballs in the pan to the preheated oven.
8. Bake the meatballs for 20 minutes in an oven at 375 deg. F.
9. Serve fresh and warm.

Per serving: Calories: 127kcal; Fat: 0.14oz; Carbs: 0.49oz; Protein: 0.32oz; Sodium: 129mg; Potassium: 0.0052oz; Phosphorus: 0.0031oz

179. Spicy Guacamole

Preparation time: 15 minutes

Cooking time: 15 minutes

Servings: 4 (about 3 tablespoons per serving)

Ingredients:

- 1½ tablespoons freshly squeezed lime juice
- 1 tablespoon minced jalapeño pepper, or to taste
- 1 tablespoon minced red onion
- 1 tablespoon chopped fresh cilantro
- 1 garlic clove, minced
- 1/8 to ¼ teaspoon kosher salt
- Freshly ground black pepper

Directions:

1. Combine the lime juice, jalapeño, onion, cilantro, garlic, salt, and pepper in a huge bowl, and mix well.

Per serving: Calories: 61kcal; Fat: 0.18oz; Carbs: 0.14oz; Protein: 0.56oz; Sodium: 123mg; Potassium: 0.0069oz; Phosphorus: 0.0054oz

180. Baked Apple Chips

Preparation time: 10 minutes

Cooking time: 2 hours

Servings: 4

Ingredients:

- 2 apples, cored and thinly sliced
- 1 teaspoon ground cinnamon
- 1/2 teaspoon granulated sugar (optional)

Directions:

1. Preheat the oven to 200 deg. F then line a baking sheet with parchment paper.
2. In your bowl, toss the apple slices with ground cinnamon and sugar (if using), making sure they are evenly coated.
3. Place the apple slices in one even layer on the baking sheet that has been prepared.
4. Cook the apple slices for 1 hour, then turn them over then continue baking for extra hour, or until the chips become crispy and have a light brown color.
5. Let cool completely before serving as a healthy and naturally sweet snack.

Per serving: Calories: 60kcal; Fat: 0oz; Carbs: 0.56oz; Protein: 0oz; Sodium: 0mg; Potassium: 0.0032oz; Phosphorus: 0.0004oz

Chapter 10.   Desserts

181. Mixed Berry Cobbler

Preparation time: 15 minutes

Cooking time: 4 hours

Servings: 8

Ingredients:

- 1/4 cup coconut almond milk
- 1/4 cup ghee
- 1/4 cup honey
- 1/2 cup almond flour
- 1/2 cup tapioca starch
- 1/2 tablespoon cinnamon
- 1/2 tablespoon coconut sugar
- 1 teaspoon vanilla
- 12 ounces frozen raspberries
- 16 ounces frozen wild blueberries
- 2 teaspoon baking powder
- 2 teaspoon tapioca starch

Directions:

1. Place the frozen berries in the slow cooker. Add honey and 2 teaspoons of tapioca starch. Mix to combine.
2. In a bowl, mix the tapioca starch, almond flour, coconut almond milk, ghee, baking powder and vanilla. Sweeten with sugar. Place this pastry mix on top of the berries.
3. Set the slow cooker for 4 hours.

Per serving: Calories: 146kcal; Fat: 0.11oz; Carbs: 1.16oz; Protein: 0.035oz; Sodium: 4mg; Potassium: 0.0047oz; Phosphorus: 0.0010oz

182. Frozen Fantasy

Preparation time: 15 minutes

Cooking time: 0 minutes

Servings: 4

Ingredients:

- 1 cup cranberry juice
- 1 cup fresh whole strawberries, washed and hulled
- 2 tbsp fresh lime juice
- 2 cup stevia
- 9 ice cubes
- a handful of strawberries for garnish

Directions:

1. Blend the cranberry juice, stevia, lime juice, and strawberries in a blender.
2. Blend until the batter is smooth, then add ice cubes and blend till smooth.
3. Pour into a glass and add strawberries to garnish.

Per serving: Calories: 100kcal; Fat: 0oz; Carbs: 0.85oz; Protein: 0.28oz; Sodium: 3mg; Potassium: 0.0038oz; Phosphorus: 0.0045oz

183. Chocolate Muffins

Preparation time: 10 minutes

Cooking time: 30 minutes

Servings: 10

Ingredients:

- 2 eggs, lightly beaten
- 1/2 cup cream
- 1/2 tsp vanilla
- 1 cup almond flour
- 1 tbsp baking powder, gluten-free
- 4 tbsp Swerve
- 1/2 cup unsweetened cocoa powder
- Pinch of salt

Directions:

1. Preheat the oven to 375 F.
2. Spray a muffin tray with cooking spray then set aside.
3. In your mixing bowl, mix together almond flour, baking powder, swerve, cocoa powder, and salt.
4. In a different bowl, beat eggs with cream, and vanilla.
5. Place egg mixture into the almond flour mixture and mix well.
6. Pour batter into the prepared muffin tray then bake in preheated oven for 30 minutes.
7. Serve and enjoy.

Per serving: Calories: 101kcal; Fat: 0.28oz; Carbs: 0.25oz; Protein: 0.18oz; Sodium: 78mg; Potassium: 0.0020oz; Phosphorus: 0.0026oz

184. Strawberry Tiramisu

Preparation time: 15 minutes

Cooking time: 10 minutes

Servings: 4

Ingredients:

- 4 ladyfingers
- 4 tbsp almond syrup or amaretto
- 1 cup stevia
- 1/2 vanilla pod
- 100g mascarpone
- 200g cream quark
- 1 tbsp chopped pistachios
- 200g strawberries

Directions:

1. Puree half of the strawberries with 1 tablespoon of stevia and the vanilla pulp. Cut the remaining strawberries into small pieces. Mix the mascarpone and cream quark with the remaining stevia.

2. Break the sponge fingers into pieces and divide them into four glasses. Pour almond syrup over it, then spread the strawberry puree and strawberries on top. Pour in the quark mixture and garnish with a piece of strawberry and the pistachios.

3. Let soak in the refrigerator for an hour.

Per serving: Calories: 315kcal; Fat: 0.74oz; Carbs: 0.85oz; Protein: 0.25oz; Sodium: 89mg; Potassium: 0.0065oz; Phosphorus: 0.0054oz

185. Fruit Salad

Preparation time: 15 minutes

Cooking time: 0 minutes

Servings: 10

Ingredients:

- 1 cup canned pineapple chunks, drained
- 2 cups canned fruit cocktail, drained
- 1 cup sliced or whole strawberries hulled
- 1 cup marshmallows
- 1 cup peeled, cored, and chopped apple

- 1/2 cup non-diary whipped topping

Directions:

1. Mix all the fruits in a bowl. Add the whipped topping and marshmallows. Mix well. Refrigerate for at least an hour. Serve chilled!

Per serving: Calories: 57kcal; Fat: 0oz; Carbs: 0.49oz; Protein: 0.035oz; Sodium: 9mg; Potassium: 0.0042oz; Phosphorus: 0.0005oz

186. Sandy Cake

Preparation time: 1 hour

Cooking time: 50 minutes

Servings: 6

Ingredients:

- 2 ½ cups starch
- 1 ½ cups oil
- 3 cups stevia
- 3 whole eggs
- 2 teaspoons half a sachet yeast

Directions:

1. In a bowl, combine the starch, whole eggs and oil, and stevia.

2. Add the well-dissolved yeast and mix until the mixture becomes uniform.

3. Pour the mixture into the pan then put it in the oven.

4. Cooking time 40-50 min at 365 deg. F.

Per serving: Calories: 589kcal; Fat: 1.06oz; Carbs: 2.79oz; Protein: 1.02oz; Sodium: 54mg; Potassium: 0.0072oz; Phosphorus: 0.0028oz

187. Chocolate Beet Cake

Preparation time: 15 minutes

Cooking time: 50 minutes

Servings: 12

Ingredients:

- 3 cups grated beets
- 1/4 cup canola oil
- 4 eggs
- 4 oz. unsweetened chocolate
- 2 tsp. phosphorus-free baking powder
- 2 cups all-purpose flour
- 1 cup stevia

Directions:

1. Set your oven to 325 F. Grease two 8-inch cake pans. Mix the baking powder, flour, and stevia. Set aside.
2. Chop the chocolate and dissolve using a double boiler. A microwave can also be used, but don't let it burn.
3. Allow it to cool, and then mix in the oil and eggs. Mix all of the wet fixings into the flour mixture and combine everything until well mixed.
4. Fold the beets in and pour the batter into the cake pans. Let them bake for 40 to 50 minutes. To know it's done, the toothpick should come out clean when inserted into the cake.
5. Remove, then allow them to cool. Once cool, invert over a plate to remove. It is great when served with whipped cream and fresh berries. Enjoy!

Per serving: Calories: 270kcal; Fat: 0.60oz; Carbs: 1.09oz; Protein: 0.21oz; Sodium: 109mg; Potassium: 0.0106oz; Phosphorus: 0.0039oz

188. Small Chocolate Cakes

Preparation time: 15 minutes
Cooking time: 1 minute
Servings: 2
Ingredients:

- 1 box of angel food cake mix
- 1 box lemon cake mix
- Water
- Nonstick cooking spray or batter
- Dark chocolate small squared chops and chocolate powder

Directions:

1. Use a transparent kitchen cooking bag and put inside both lemon cake mixes, angel food mix, and chocolate squared chops. Mix everything and put water to prepare a small cupcake.
2. Put the mix in a mold to prepare a cupcake containing the ingredients and put in microwave for a one-minute high temperature.
3. Slip the cupcake out of the mold, put it on a dish, let it cool, and put some more chocolate crumbs on it. Serve and enjoy!

Per serving: Calories: 95kcal; Fat: 0.11oz; Carbs: 0.99oz; Protein: 0.035oz; Sodium: 162mg; Potassium: 0.0005oz; Phosphorus: 0.0028oz

189. Strawberry Pie

Preparation time: 15 minutes
Cooking time: 20 minutes
Servings: 8
Ingredients:

For the Crust:

- 1 1/2 cups Graham cracker crumbs
- 5 tbsp oil, at room temperature
- 4 tbsp. stevia

For the Pie:

- 1 1/2 tsp gelatin powder
- 3 tbsp cornstarch
- 2 cup stevia
- 5 cups sliced strawberries, divided
- 1 cup water

Directions:

1. For the crust: heat your oven to 375 deg. F. Grease a pie pan. Combine the oil, crumbs, and stevia and then press them into your pie pan.
2. Bake the crust within 10 to 15 minutes, until lightly browned. Take out of the oven and let it cool completely.
3. For the pie, crush up a cup of strawberries. Using a small pot, combine the stevia, water, gelatin, and cornstarch. Bring the mixture in the pot up to a boil, lower the heat, and simmer until it has thickened.
4. Add in the crushed strawberries in the pot and let it simmer for another 5 minutes until the sauce has thickened up again. Set it off the heat and pour it into a bowl. Cool until it comes to room temperature.
5. Toss the remaining berries with the sauce to be well distributed, pour into the pie crust, and spread it into an even layer. Refrigerate the pie until cold. It will take about 3 hours. Serve and enjoy!

Per serving: Calories: 265kcal; Fat: 0.25oz; Carbs: 1.69oz; Protein: 0.11oz; Sodium: 143mg; Potassium: 0.0065oz; Phosphorus: 0.0016oz

190. Fruit Crunch

Preparation time: 15 minutes

Cooking time: 35 minutes

Servings: 8

Ingredients:

- 4 tart apples, pare, core and slice
- 2 cup stevia
- 1/2 cup sifted all-purpose flour
- 1/3 cup margarine, softened
- 3/4 cup rolled oats
- 3/4 tsp nutmeg

Directions:

1. Preheat your oven to 375 deg.. Place the apples in a greased square 8-inch pan.
2. Mix the other ingredients in a medium-sized bowl and spread the mixture over the apple.
3. Bake within 35 minutes or until the Apple turns lightly brown and tender.

Per serving: Calories: 217kcal; Fat: 0.21oz; Carbs: 1.27oz; Protein: 0.071oz; Sodium: 62mg; Potassium: 0.0024oz; Phosphorus: 0.0013oz

191. Blueberry Espresso Brownies

Preparation time: 15 minutes

Cooking time: 30 minutes

Servings: 12

Ingredients:

- 1/4 cup organic cocoa powder
- 1/4 teaspoon salt
- 1/2 cup raw honey
- 1/2 teaspoon baking soda
- 1 cup blueberries
- 1 cup coconut cream
- 1 tablespoon cinnamon
- 1 tablespoon ground coffee
- 2 teaspoon vanilla extract
- 3 eggs

Directions:

1. Preheat the oven to 325 deg. F.
2. In a bow mix together coconut cream, honey, eggs, cinnamon, honey, vanilla, baking soda, coffee and salt.
3. Use a mixer to combine all ingredients.

4. Fold in the blueberries
5. Transfer the batter in a greased baking dish and bake for 30 minutes or 'til a toothpick inserted in the middle comes out clean.
6. Remove from the oven then let it cool.

Per serving: Calories: 168kcal; Fat: 0.35oz; Carbs: 0.71oz; Protein: 0.14oz; Sodium: 129mg; Potassium: 0.0060oz; Phosphorus: 0.0028oz

192. Frozen Lemon Dessert

Preparation time: 15 minutes

Cooking time: 10 minutes

Servings: 6

Ingredients:

- 4 eggs, separated
- 1/4 cup lemon juice
- 3 cup stevia
- 1 tbsp lemon peel, grated
- 2 cups vanilla wafers, crushed
- 1 cup whipping cream, whipped

Directions:

1. Beat the egg yolks until it becomes very thick. Slowly add stevia and beat each time you add. Put the lemon peel plus lemon juice, mix well.
2. Put the batter in your double boiler, then cook over boiling water, continually stirring until the mixture gets thick. Set aside to cool.
3. Mix the egg whites until stiff peaks. Fold the egg whites into the thick mixture once cooled.
4. Add whipped cream and fold in. Spread one and a half crumbs of the vanilla wafer in the bottom of a baking dish or freezer tray.
5. Scoop the lemon mixture and spread over the crumbs. Sprinkle the remaining vanilla wafer crumbs on the top. Fridge for several hours until the mixture is firm.

Per serving: Calories: 205kcal; Fat: 0.21oz; Carbs: 1.13oz; Protein: 0.11oz; Sodium: 97mg; Potassium: 0.0024oz; Phosphorus: 0.0012oz

193. Pineapple Cake

Preparation time: 30 minutes

Cooking time: 45 minutes

Servings: 6

Ingredients:

FOR THE BASE:

- ¾ cup of flour
- 2 eggs
- 1 ½ cups of stevia
- 2 teaspoons of vanilla yeast

FOR THE CREAM:

- 1 whole egg, 1 yolk
- 1 cup stevia
- 3 tablespoons flour
- 2 cups semi-skimmed milk
- 1 cup pineapple
- 1 ½ cups cream for desserts
- Grated lemon zest

Directions:

1. To prepare the base of the cake you have to work flour, stevia, yeast until a homogeneous mixture. Bake at 160 deg. for about 15 minutes. After baking, let the cake cool.

2. Meanwhile, prepare the cream. In a saucepan, place on low heat, beat a whole egg, and the yolk with the stevia and flour.

3. Add the milk lukewarm previously brought to a boil with 1/2 grated lemon zest.

4. Cook everything on a slow fire, continuing to stir for about 4-5 minutes.

5. When the base has cooled, cut the part upper (2/3 sup.). Pour on the bottom the pineapple juice (from the can), then put the prepared cream and a layer of cream.

6. Finally, cover them with the mixture obtained from crumbling of the unused part of the cake (the smaller one) combined with the pineapple cut into small pieces.

7. Before serving, the cake must be in the fridge for 2 hours.

Per serving: Calories: 423kcal; Fat: 0.60oz; Carbs: 2.15oz; Protein: 0.35oz; Sodium: 97mg; Potassium: 0.0131oz; Phosphorus: 0.0068oz

194. Spritz Cookies

Preparation time: 15 minutes

Cooking time: 8 minutes

Servings: 75 cookies

Ingredients:

- 5 cups all-purpose flour
- 2 cup + 4 tbsp stevia
- 2 cups oil - 2 eggs
- 1 tsp almond extract
- 2 tsp vanilla extract

Directions:

1. Preheat your oven to 400 deg.. Mix oil, flour, and stevia together. Put the vanilla almond extract and the eggs.

2. Mix the ingredients using a hand mixer on low speed. Put cookie batter into an ungreased baking sheet. Bake for about 8 minutes. Allow cooling before you serve.

Per serving: Calories: 172kcal; Fat: 0oz; Carbs: 0.92oz; Protein: 0.071oz; Sodium: 56mg; Potassium: 0.0010oz; Phosphorus: 0.0008oz

195. Sweet Raspberry Candy

Preparation time: 5 minutes

Cooking time: 5 minutes

Servings: 12

Ingredients:

- 1/2 cup dried raspberries
- 3 tbsp Swerve
- 1/2 cup coconut oil
- 2 oz cacao oil
- 1/2 tsp vanilla

Directions:

1. Add cacao oil and coconut oil in a saucepan and melt over low heat. Remove from heat.

2. Grind the raspberries in a food processor.

3. Add sweetener and ground raspberries into the melted oil and coconut oil mixture and stir well.

4. Pour mixture into the mini silicone candy molds and place them in the refrigerator until set.

5. Serve and enjoy.

Per serving: Calories: 103kcal; Fat: 0.39oz; Carbs: 0.035oz; Protein: 0.0035oz; Sodium: 45mg; Potassium: 0.0043oz; Phosphorus: 0.0034oz

196. Gumdrop Cookies

Preparation time: 15 minutes

Cooking time: 12 minutes

Servings: 25

Ingredients:

- ½ cup of spreadable unsalted butter
- 1 medium egg
- 1 cup of brown sugar
- 1 2/3 cups of all-purpose flour, sifted
- ¼ cup of almond milk
- 1 teaspoon vanilla
- 1 teaspoon of baking powder
- 15 large gumdrops, chopped finely

Directions:

1. Preheat the oven at 400 deg. F.
2. Combine the sugar, butter and egg until creamy.
3. Add the almond milk and vanilla then stir well.
4. Mix the flour with the baking powder in a different bowl. Incorporate to the sugar, butter mixture, and stir.
5. Add the gumdrops and place the mixture in the fridge for half an hour.
6. Drop the dough with tablespoonful into a lightly greased baking or cookie sheet.
7. Bake for 10-12 minutes or 'til golden brown.

Per serving: Calories: 102.17kcal; Fat: 0.14oz; Carbs: 0.58oz; Protein: 0.030oz; Sodium: 23.42mg; Potassium: 0.0016oz; Phosphorus: 0.0011oz

197. Watermelon Mint Granita

Preparation time: 10 minutes + chilling time

Cooking time: 0 minutes

Servings: 2

Ingredients:

- 2 cups watermelon cubes, seeded
- 1/8 cup sugar
- 1 tbsp freshly squeezed lemon juice
- 1 tbsp minced fresh mint leaves

Directions:

1. In a food processor or blender, combine the watermelon, sugar, lemon juice, and mint and blend until smooth.
2. Pour the mixture into your 9-inch square pan. Freeze for 2 hours, stirring the mixture once during freezing time.
3. To serve, scrape some granita with a fork and lightly spoon it into glasses.

Per serving: Calories: 81kcal; Fat: 0oz; Carbs: 0.74oz; Protein: 0.035oz; Sodium: 1mg; Potassium: 0.0043oz; Phosphorus: 0.0004oz

198. Jeweled Cookies

Preparation time: 15 minutes

Cooking time: 10 minutes

Servings: 50 cookies

Ingredients:

- 1/2 cup softened unsalted margarine or oil
- 1 3/4 cup sifted all-purpose flour
- 2 cup stevia
- 1 medium egg
- 1 tsp vanilla
- 1/4 cup milk
- 1 tsp baking powder
- 15 large gumdrops

Directions:

1. Preheat your oven to 400 deg.. Mix the egg, oil, and stevia thoroughly in a bowl. Add in vanilla and milk, then stir.
2. Mix the flour plus baking powder in a different bowl. Add to the previous mixture. Now add the gumdrops and stir, then chill for a minimum of one hour.
3. Spoon the dough using a tablespoon, then put it on an oiled cookie sheet. Bake for approximately 10 minutes or until it turns golden brown.

Per serving: Calories: 104kcal; Fat: 0.21oz; Carbs: 0.78oz; Protein: 0.035oz; Sodium: 9mg; Potassium: 0.0010oz; Phosphorus: 0.0006oz

199. Ribbon Cakes

Preparation time: 15 minutes

Cooking time: 30 minutes

Servings: 2

Ingredients:

- 3 cups unsoftened all-purpose flour
- 2 whole eggs
- 2 cup stevia
- 1 tsp baking powder
- Jelly or jam like apricot jam/raspberry jelly
- 1 cup margarine or oil, softened

- 1 egg white
- 1/2 tsp vanilla
- 1 cup blackberry or plum

Directions:

1. Heat your oven to 375 deg. F. Mix the stevia, flour, and baking powder in a bowl. Blend the oil using a pastry blender or your fingertips 'til the mixture looks like cornmeal.

2. Add egg white, eggs, and vanilla into the mixture and work into a stiff dough. Split the dough into two, with one part being twice the size of the other.

3. Spread about ¼ to ½ cups of flour on a board and roll out the bigger ball to approximately 1/8 inch thickness.

4. Put the rolled dough in a cookie pan and smoothen the edges. Spread the jelly/ jam on top. Roll out the leftover dough to the same thickness and cut it into half-inch wide strips.

5. Place the strips diagonally across the jam or jelly, half-inch apart. Put the stevia over the top of the dough and put it into the oven.

6. When the edges begin to brown after 20 minutes, remove and cut off about 3 inches around all the edges.

7. Take out the cut-off parts and place the pan back into the oven for approximately 10 minutes. Cut into 1-inch by 2-inches rectangles to give you seven dozen cookies.

Per serving: Calories: 106kcal; Fat: 0oz; Carbs: 0.53oz; Protein: 0.035oz; Sodium: 65mg; Potassium: 0.0006oz; Phosphorus: 0.0010oz

200. Lemon Cake

Preparation time: 15 minutes

Cooking time: 1 hour & 20 minutes

Servings: 12

Ingredients:

- 2 cups oil
- 8 cups stevia
- 2 tsp grated lemon zest
- 1 tsp lemon extract
- 6 eggs
- 3 1/2 cup sifted all-purpose flour

Directions:

1. Preheat your oven to 350 deg.. Cream oil on low speed with an electric mixer until light and fluffy.

2. Slowly add in stevia and lemon zest; mix thoroughly. Add lemon extract and the eggs, one at a time, mixing after each addition.

3. Add flour gradually and mix well. Pour batter into a greased & floured pan. Bake for one hour, 20 minutes. You will know it is done when a toothpick inserted in the cake center comes out clean.

Per serving: Calories: 279kcal; Fat: 0oz; Carbs: 1.20oz; Protein: 0.35oz; Sodium: 127mg; Potassium: 0.0038oz; Phosphorus: 0.0049oz

BONUS

BONUS 1:

I'm delighted to reveal a special gift, tucked right inside your already purchased "Kidney Diet Cookbook for Beginners." Because you deserve an experience that lifts your culinary journey off the pages; you deserve to witness the beauty and color of what you'll be bringing to your table. That's why, within the book you've chosen, you'll find an exclusive version featuring full-color photographs of the ready dishes, a true feast for the eyes even before it delights your palate. This is not just a thank you for choosing me but a symbol of our shared journey towards wellness, celebrating every dish that marries taste and health..

BONUS 2:

I'm excited to introduce a phenomenal bonus that accompanies the "Kidney Diet Cookbook for Beginners". This unique addition is not just a supplement; it's a complete guide that complements the rich content of the cookbook. While the main book offers a wide range of recipes and dietary advice suitable for kidney health, this bonus material provides an in-depth exploration of lifestyle changes, habits, and essential practices for managing kidney health.

In this special bonus, we delve into understanding the different types of kidney diseases and their current treatments, offering valuable insights for those dealing with the complexities of kidney health. It's a holistic approach that goes beyond nutrition, addressing critical aspects of lifestyle and daily habits that impact kidney health.

Moreover, the bonus content includes guidance on do's and don'ts for optimal kidney care, providing you with practical knowledge to make informed decisions about your health. We'll cover everything from stress management and exercise to understanding the complexities of various kidney conditions.

By integrating this bonus with the "Kidney Diet Cookbook for Beginners", we aim to provide a 360-degree view of managing kidney health. It's not just about what you eat; it's about embracing a lifestyle that supports kidney health. This bonus is our gift to you, a testament to our commitment to offering comprehensive support and information to those embarking on their journey towards improving kidney health. With this book and its bonus content, you're not just receiving recipes; you're gaining a partner in your journey towards wellness.

You can download these bonus by scanning the QR code

BONUS 3: Vegan Recipes

Kidney diseases can affect individuals with various dietary lifestyles, including those who follow a vegan diet. It's a common misconception that a diet high in vegetables and low in animal proteins is automatically healthier and less taxing on the kidneys. However, vegan diets can also pose challenges for kidney health if not carefully balanced.

Firstly, not all vegan foods are low in sodium, phosphorus, and potassium, nutrients that often need to be monitored and regulated in the presence of kidney diseases. Some meat substitutes, for example, can be highly processed and contain high amounts of added salt and phosphates. Whole foods like legumes, nuts, and certain types of fruits and vegetables can also be high in potassium.

Moreover, the notion of "needing to lose weight" to improve kidney health is not always the correct approach. While maintaining a healthy body weight is important, weight loss must be managed carefully, ensuring the diet provides all essential nutrients without overburdening the kidneys. Consequently, losing weight through extreme or unbalanced diets can exacerbate kidney problems rather than resolve them.

Thus, while a vegan diet can be part of a healthy and sustainable lifestyle, it's essential for vegans to consider the proper balance of nutrients in their diet. The key to supporting kidney health is a well-planned diet that accounts for individual nutritional needs and is low in those foods that can strain kidney function.

Chapter 11.   Vegan Breakfast Recipes

201. Vegan Tofu Scramble Breakfast Tacos

Preparation time: 10 minutes

Cooking time: 10 minutes

Servings: 2

Ingredients:

- 1/2 block firm tofu, crumbled
- 1/4 teaspoon turmeric
- 1/4 teaspoon garlic powder
- 1/4 teaspoon onion powder
- 1/4 teaspoon paprika
- Salt and pepper to taste (low-sodium)
- 4 small corn tortillas
- 1/2 avocado, sliced
- Fresh cilantro for garnish

Directions:

1. In your skillet, heat olive oil over medium heat. Add crumbled tofu and cook for 3-4 minutes until slightly golden.
2. Stir in turmeric, garlic powder, onion powder, paprika, salt, and pepper. Cook for another 2-3 minutes.
3. Warm the corn tortillas in your dry skillet or microwave.
4. Divide the tofu scramble among the tortillas. Top with sliced avocado and fresh cilantro.
5. Serve the tacos hot.

Per serving: Calories: 220kcal; Fat: 0.39oz; Carbs: 0.71oz; Protein: 0.39oz; Sodium: 20mg; Potassium: 0.0113oz; Phosphorus: 0.0065oz

202. Vegetable Tofu Scramble

Preparation time: 10 minutes

Cooking time: 15 minutes

Servings: 2

Ingredients:

- 1 tablespoon olive oil
- 1/2 onion, diced
- 1/2 bell pepper, diced
- 1/2 zucchini, diced
- 1/2 cup firm tofu, crumbled
- 1/4 teaspoon turmeric
- Salt and pepper to taste (low-sodium)
- Fresh parsley for garnish

Directions:

1. In your skillet, heat olive oil over medium heat. Add onion, bell pepper, and zucchini. Sauté for 5 minutes until softened.
2. Add crumbled tofu and turmeric. Cook for another 5 minutes, stirring occasionally.
3. Season with salt and pepper.
4. Serve hot, garnished with fresh parsley.

Per serving: Calories: 160kcal; Fat: 0.32oz; Carbs: 0.32oz; Protein: 0.42oz; Sodium: 20mg; Potassium: 0.0083oz; Phosphorus: 0.0053oz

203. Oatmeal with Apples and Cinnamon

Preparation time: 5 minutes

Cooking time: 10 minutes

Servings: 2

Ingredients:

- 1 cup rolled oats
- 2 cups water
- 1 apple, peeled and diced
- 1/2 teaspoon cinnamon
- 1 tablespoon almond butter (low-sodium)
- Stevia (optional)

Directions:

1. In your saucepan, bring the water to a boil.
2. Add the rolled oats, diced apple, and cinnamon. Reduce heat then simmer for 5-7 minutes, stirring occasionally.
3. Divide the oatmeal into two bowls and top with almond butter.
4. Sweeten with stevia, if desired.

Per serving: Calories: 235kcal; Fat: 0.25oz; Carbs: 1.38oz; Protein: 0.21oz; Sodium: 5mg; Potassium: 0.0058oz; Phosphorus: 0.0035oz

204. Vegan Breakfast Quinoa Bars

Preparation time: 10 minutes

Cooking time: 25 minutes

Servings: 8

Ingredients:

- 1 cup cooked quinoa
- 1/2 cup rolled oats
- 1/4 cup chopped almonds
- 1/4 cup dried cranberries
- 2 tablespoons maple syrup (low-sodium)
- 1 tablespoon almond butter (low-sodium)
- 1/2 teaspoon vanilla extract

Directions:

1. Preheat the oven to 350 deg. F. Grease a baking dish.
2. In a bowl, combine cooked quinoa, rolled oats, chopped almonds, and dried cranberries.
3. In a small saucepan, heat maple syrup, almond butter, and vanilla extract until well combined.
4. Pour the syrup mixture over the quinoa mixture and stir until everything is evenly coated.
5. Press the mixture into your greased baking dish.
6. Bake for 20-25 minutes 'til the bars are golden brown.
7. Let the bars to cool before cutting into squares.

Per serving: Calories: 130kcal; Fat: 0.14oz; Carbs: 0.71oz; Protein: 0.11oz; Sodium: 10mg; Potassium: 0.0034oz; Phosphorus: 0.0025oz

205. Vegan Breakfast Burrito

Preparation time: 10 minutes

Cooking time: 10 minutes

Servings: 2

Ingredients:

- 4 small corn tortillas
- 1/2 cup black beans (low-sodium), cooked and mashed
- 1/2 avocado, sliced
- 1/4 cup salsa (low-sodium)
- Fresh cilantro for garnish

Directions:

1. Warm the corn tortillas in your dry skillet or microwave.

2. Spread mashed black beans on each tortilla and top with avocado slices and salsa.
3. Roll up the tortillas and serve.
4. Garnish with fresh cilantro.

Per serving: Calories: 240kcal; Fat: 0.35oz; Carbs: 1.24oz; Protein: 0.28oz; Sodium: 15mg; Potassium: 0.0101oz; Phosphorus: 0.0042oz

206. Vegan Breakfast Quinoa Salad

Preparation time: 10 minutes

Cooking time: 15 minutes

Servings: 2

Ingredients:

- 1 cup cooked quinoa
- 1/2 cup diced cucumber
- 1/2 cup diced tomatoes
- 1/4 cup diced red onion
- 2 tablespoons chopped fresh parsley
- 1 tablespoon lemon juice
- 1 tablespoon olive oil
- Salt and pepper to taste (low-sodium)

Directions:

1. In a bowl, combine cooked quinoa, diced cucumber, tomatoes, red onion, and chopped parsley.
2. In a small jar, combine lemon juice, olive oil, salt, and pepper. Shake well to emulsify the dressing.
3. Transfer the dressing over the quinoa salad then toss to coat evenly.
4. Serve chilled or at room temperature.

Per serving: Calories: 190kcal; Fat: 0.25oz; Carbs: 0.95oz; Protein: 0.18oz; Sodium: 10mg; Potassium: 0.0087oz; Phosphorus: 0.0037oz

207. Vegan Tofu Benedict

Preparation time: 10 minutes

Cooking time: 20 minutes

Servings: 2

Ingredients:

- 1 block firm tofu, sliced into 4 rectangles
- 2 English muffins, split and toasted
- 2 cups fresh spinach
- 1/2 cup unsweetened almond milk (low-sodium)

- 1 tablespoon nutritional yeast
- 1/2 teaspoon turmeric
- Salt and pepper to taste (low-sodium)
- Lemon wedges for garnish

Directions:

1. In your skillet, heat olive oil over medium heat. Add tofu slices and cook for 4-5 minutes on each side until golden brown.
2. In a blender, combine almond milk, nutritional yeast, turmeric, salt, and pepper. Blend until smooth.
3. In the same skillet, wilt the spinach. Add the blended mixture to the skillet then cook for 2 minutes until heated through.
4. Assemble the Benedict by placing a tofu slice on each toasted English muffin half. Spoon the spinach mixture on top.
5. Serve with lemon wedges on the side.

Per serving: Calories: 230kcal; Fat: 0.32oz; Carbs: 0.85oz; Protein: 0.56oz; Sodium: 25mg; Potassium: 0.0131oz; Phosphorus: 0.0079oz

208. Sweet Potato Toast

Preparation time: 5 minutes

Cooking time: 20 minutes

Servings: 2

Ingredients:

- 1 large sweet potato, sliced lengthwise into 1/4-inch thick slices
- 2 tablespoons almond butter (low-sodium)
- 1 tablespoon chopped walnuts
- Cinnamon (optional)

Directions:

1. Preheat the oven to 400 deg. F. Bring the sweet potato slices on a baking sheet lined with parchment paper.
2. Bake for 15-20 minutes 'til the slices are tender and slightly crispy.
3. Spread almond butter on each slice and top with chopped walnuts.
4. Sprinkle with cinnamon, if desired.

Per serving: Calories: 210kcal; Fat: 0.28oz; Carbs: 1.06oz; Protein: 0.18oz; Sodium: 30mg; Potassium: 0.0138oz; Phosphorus: 0.0033oz

209. Fruit Salad with Coconut Yogurt

Preparation time: 10 minutes

Cooking time: 0 minutes

Servings: 2

Ingredients:

- 1 cup mixed fresh fruit (e.g., berries, melon, grapes)
- 1/2 cup coconut yogurt (low-sodium)
- 2 tablespoons chopped almonds

Directions:

1. Wash and chop the fresh fruit.
2. In a bowl, combine the fruit and coconut yogurt.
3. Sprinkle with chopped almonds.
4. Serve chilled.

Per serving: Calories: 160kcal; Fat: 0.25oz; Carbs: 0.81oz; Protein: 0.14oz; Sodium: 15mg; Potassium: 0.0065oz; Phosphorus: 0.0030oz

210. Vegan Blueberry Muffins

Preparation time: 10 minutes

Cooking time: 20 minutes

Servings: 12

Ingredients:

- 2 cups whole wheat flour
- 2 teaspoons baking powder
- 1/2 teaspoon baking soda
- 1/4 teaspoon salt (low-sodium)
- 1/2 cup maple syrup (low-sodium)
- 1 cup unsweetened almond milk (low-sodium)
- 1/4 cup melted coconut oil
- 1 teaspoon vanilla extract
- 1 cup fresh or frozen blueberries

Directions:

1. Preheat the oven to 375 deg. F. Grease your muffin tin or line with muffin liners.
2. In your mixing bowl, combine whole wheat flour, baking powder, baking soda, and salt.
3. In a separate bowl, mix maple syrup, almond milk, melted coconut oil, and vanilla extract.
4. Place the wet ingredients to the dry ingredients then mix until just combined. Fold in the blueberries.
5. Place the batter evenly among the muffin cups.

6. Bake for 18-20 minutes 'til a toothpick inserted into the center comes out clean.

7. Allow the muffins to cool before serving.

Per serving: Calories: 160kcal; Fat: 0.18oz; Carbs: 0.92oz; Protein: 0.11oz; Sodium: 50mg; Potassium: 0.0042oz; Phosphorus: 0.0030oz

211. Vegan Zucchini Fritters

Preparation time: 15 minutes

Cooking time: 15 minutes

Servings: 2

Ingredients:

- 2 medium zucchini, grated
- 1/4 cup chickpea flour
- 2 tablespoons nutritional yeast
- 2 tablespoons chopped fresh parsley
- 1/2 teaspoon garlic powder
- 1/4 teaspoon onion powder
- Salt and pepper to taste (low-sodium)
- Olive oil for frying

Directions:

1. Place the grated zucchini in a colander then sprinkle with salt. Let it sit for 10 minutes to draw out excess moisture.

2. Squeeze the grated zucchini to take as much liquid as possible. Transfer it to a mixing bowl.

3. Add chickpea flour, nutritional yeast, parsley, garlic powder, onion powder, salt, and pepper to the grated zucchini. Stir well to combine.

4. Heat olive oil in your skillet in a medium heat. Scoop spoonfuls of the zucchini mixture into the skillet and flatten them with a spatula.

5. Cook the fritters for 3-4 mins on each side 'til golden brown and crispy.

6. Serve the zucchini fritters hot with a side of vegan yogurt or a dipping sauce of your choice.

Per serving: Calories: 130kcal; Fat: 0.14oz; Carbs: 0.64oz; Protein: 0.32oz; Sodium: 20mg; Potassium: 0.0131oz; Phosphorus: 0.0085oz

212. Vegan Breakfast Couscous

Preparation time: 5 minutes

Cooking time: 5 minutes

Servings: 2

Ingredients:

- 1 cup cooked couscous
- 1/4 cup chopped almonds
- 2 tablespoons dried cranberries
- 1 tablespoon maple syrup (low-sodium)
- 1/2 teaspoon cinnamon
- 1/4 teaspoon vanilla extract
- Unsweetened almond milk (low-sodium), for serving

Directions:

1. In a bowl, combine cooked couscous, chopped almonds, dried cranberries, maple syrup, cinnamon, and vanilla extract. Stir well.

2. Serve the breakfast couscous with a splash of almond milk.

Per serving: Calories: 240kcal; Fat: 0.25oz; Carbs: 1.38oz; Protein: 0.21oz; Sodium: 10mg; Potassium: 0.0058oz; Phosphorus: 0.0042oz

213. Vegan Tofu Breakfast Burrito Bowl

Preparation time: 10 minutes

Cooking time: 20 minutes

Servings: 2

Ingredients:

- 1 cup cooked brown rice
- 1/2 block firm tofu, crumbled
- 1/2 teaspoon turmeric
- 1/4 teaspoon garlic powder
- 1/4 teaspoon onion powder
- 1/4 teaspoon paprika
- Salt and pepper to taste (low-sodium)
- 1/2 avocado, sliced
- Fresh cilantro for garnish

Directions:

1. In your skillet, heat olive oil over medium heat. Add crumbled tofu and cook for 3-4 minutes until slightly golden.

2. Stir in turmeric, garlic powder, onion powder, paprika, salt, and pepper. Cook for another 2-3 minutes.

3. Divide the cooked brown rice into two bowls. Top with the tofu scramble, sliced avocado, and fresh cilantro.

4. Serve hot.

Per serving: Calories: 280kcal; Fat: 0.49oz; Carbs: 1.02oz; Protein: 0.42oz; Sodium: 15mg; Potassium: 0.0126oz; Phosphorus: 0.0065oz

214. Vegan Overnight Oats

Preparation time: 5 minutes

Cooking time: Overnight (chill time)

Servings: 2

Ingredients:

- 1 cup rolled oats
- 1 cup unsweetened almond milk (low-sodium)
- 1 tablespoon chia seeds
- 1 tablespoon maple syrup (low-sodium)
- 1/2 teaspoon vanilla extract
- Fresh berries for topping

Directions:

1. In a bowl, combine rolled oats, almond milk, chia seeds, maple syrup, and vanilla extract. Stir well.
2. Cover the bowl then refrigerate overnight or for at least 4 hours.
3. Stir the oats before serving and top with fresh berries.

Per serving: Calories: 200kcal; Fat: 0.25oz; Carbs: 1.06oz; Protein: 0.21oz; Sodium: 15mg; Potassium: 0.0058oz; Phosphorus: 0.0044oz

215. Vegan Breakfast Tofu Stir-Fry

Preparation time: 10 minutes

Cooking time: 15 minutes

Servings: 2

Ingredients:

- 1/2 block firm tofu, diced
- 1 cup mixed vegetables (bell peppers, mushrooms, snap peas)
- 1 tablespoon low-sodium soy sauce
- 1 tablespoon rice vinegar
- 1 teaspoon sesame oil
- 1/4 teaspoon garlic powder
- 1/4 teaspoon ginger powder
- Salt and pepper to taste (low-sodium)
- Cooked quinoa or brown rice, for serving

Directions:

1. In your skillet, heat sesame oil over medium heat. Add diced tofu and cook for 4-5 minutes until slightly browned.
2. Place the mixed vegetables to the skillet and cook for another 4-5 minutes until tender-crisp.
3. In your small bowl, whisk together soy sauce, rice vinegar, garlic powder, ginger powder, salt, and pepper.
4. Transfer the sauce over the tofu and vegetables. Stir well to coat everything evenly.
5. Serve the tofu stir-fry over cooked quinoa or brown rice.

Per serving: Calories: 230kcal; Fat: 0.32oz; Carbs: 1.06oz; Protein: 0.46oz; Sodium: 270mg; Potassium: 0.0133oz; Phosphorus: 0.0083oz

216. Vegan Tofu and Vegetable Stir-Fry

Preparation time: 10 minutes

Cooking time: 15 minutes

Servings: 2

Ingredients:

- 1/2 block firm tofu, diced
- 1 cup mixed vegetables (bell peppers, broccoli, carrots)
- 1 tablespoon low-sodium soy sauce
- 1 tablespoon maple syrup (low-sodium)
- 1 teaspoon sesame oil
- 1/4 teaspoon garlic powder
- 1/4 teaspoon ginger powder
- Salt and pepper to taste (low-sodium)
- Cooked brown rice, for serving

Directions:

1. In your skillet, heat sesame oil over medium heat. Add diced tofu and cook for 4-5 minutes until slightly browned.
2. Place the mixed vegetables to the skillet and cook for another 4-5 minutes until tender-crisp.
3. In your small bowl, whisk together soy sauce, maple syrup, garlic powder, ginger powder, salt, and pepper.
4. Transfer the sauce over the tofu and vegetables. Stir well to coat everything evenly.
5. Serve the tofu and vegetable stir-fry over cooked brown rice.

Per serving: Calories: 220kcal; Fat: 0.25oz; Carbs: 1.13oz; Protein: 0.42oz; Sodium: 250mg; Potassium: 0.0131oz; Phosphorus: 0.0079oz

217. Vegan Chickpea Flour Pancakes

Preparation time: 10 minutes

Cooking time: 15 minutes

Servings: 2

Ingredients:

- 1 cup chickpea flour
- 1 tablespoon ground flaxseed mixed + 3 tablespoons water
- 1/2 cup unsweetened almond milk (low-sodium)
- 1/2 teaspoon baking powder
- 1/4 teaspoon turmeric
- Salt and pepper to taste (low-sodium)
- Olive oil for frying
- Toppings: sliced avocado, cherry tomatoes, fresh herbs

Directions:

1. In a bowl, whisk together chickpea flour, flaxseed mixture, almond milk, baking powder, turmeric, salt, and pepper until smooth.
2. Heat olive oil in your skillet in a medium heat. Pour a ladleful of batter into the skillet and spread it into a round pancake shape.
3. Cook the pancake for 2-3 minutes on each side until golden brown and cooked through.
4. Repeat with the remaining batter to make more pancakes.
5. Serve the chickpea flour pancakes hot with sliced avocado, cherry tomatoes, and fresh herbs as toppings.

Per serving: Calories: 260kcal; Fat: 0.32oz; Carbs: 1.09oz; Protein: 0.46oz; Sodium: 10mg; Potassium: 0.0115oz; Phosphorus: 0.0090oz

218. Vegan Chia Pudding

Preparation time: 5 minutes

Cooking time: Overnight (chill time)

Servings: 2

Ingredients:

- 1/4 cup chia seeds
- 1 cup unsweetened almond milk (low-sodium)
- 1 tablespoon maple syrup (low-sodium)
- 1/2 teaspoon vanilla extract
- Fresh berries for topping

Directions:

1. In your jar or bowl, combine chia seeds, almond milk, maple syrup, and vanilla extract. Stir well.
2. Cover the jar or bowl and refrigerate overnight or for at least 4 hours.
3. Stir the chia pudding before serving and top with fresh berries.

Per serving: Calories: 160kcal; Fat: 0.28oz; Carbs: 0.64oz; Protein: 0.18oz; Sodium: 10mg; Potassium: 0.0048oz; Phosphorus: 0.0033oz

219. Stuffed Sweet Potatoes

Preparation time: 10 minutes

Cooking time: 1 hour

Servings: 4

Ingredients:

- 4 medium sweet potatoes
- 1 can black beans, rinsed and drained
- 1 cup diced bell peppers (any color)
- 1 cup corn kernels
- 1/4 cup chopped cilantro
- 2 tablespoons lime juice
- 1 teaspoon ground cumin
- 1/2 teaspoon chili powder
- Salt and pepper to taste

Directions:

1. Preheat the oven to 400 deg. F.
2. Pierce the sweet potatoes multiple times with a fork, then bring them on a baking sheet. Bake for about 45-60 minutes, or until tender.
3. In a bowl, combine the black beans, diced bell peppers, corn kernels, cilantro, lime juice, cumin, chili powder, salt, and pepper.
4. When the sweet potatoes are cooked, slice them open and stuff each one with the black bean mixture.
5. Serve hot.

Per serving: Calories: 230kcal; Fat: 0.035oz; Carbs: 1.80oz; Protein: 0.28oz; Sodium: 70mg; Potassium: 0.0106oz; Phosphorus: 0.0071oz

220. Vegan Sweet Potato Breakfast Bowl

Preparation time: 10 minutes

Cooking time: 20 minutes

Servings: 2

Ingredients:

- 1 large sweet potato, peeled and cubed
- 1 tablespoon olive oil
- 1/2 teaspoon paprika
- 1/4 teaspoon garlic powder
- 1/4 teaspoon onion powder
- Salt and pepper to taste (low-sodium)
- 1/4 cup cooked quinoa
- 2 tablespoons chopped almonds
- 2 tablespoons dried cranberries
- 2 tablespoons maple syrup (low-sodium)

Directions:

1. Preheat the oven to 400 deg. F.
2. In your bowl, toss the cubed sweet potato with olive oil, paprika, garlic powder, onion powder, salt, and pepper.
3. Spread the sweet potato cubes into single layer on a baking sheet. Bake for 20 minutes until tender and slightly caramelized.
4. Divide the cooked quinoa between two bowls. Top with roasted sweet potato cubes, chopped almonds, and dried cranberries.
5. Drizzle maple syrup over the sweet potato breakfast bowls.

Per serving: Calories: 270kcal; Fat: 0.28oz; Carbs: 1.69oz; Protein: 0.18oz; Sodium: 20mg; Potassium: 0.0113oz; Phosphorus: 0.0048oz

Chapter 12.   Vegan Meal Recipes

221. Vegetarian Gobi Curry

Preparation time: 20 minutes

Cooking time: 15 minutes

Servings: 2

Ingredients:

- 1 cups cauliflower floret
- 1 tbsp unsalted butter
- 1/2 medium dry white onion, thinly chopped
- 1/4 cup green peas
- 1/2 tsp fresh ginger, chopped
- 1/4 tsp turmeric
- 1/2 tsp garam masala
- 1/8 tsp cayenne pepper
- 1/2 tbsp water

Directions:

1. Heat your skillet over medium heat with the butter and sauté the onions until caramelized.
2. Add the ginger, garam masala, turmeric, and cayenne. Add the cauliflower and peas then stir well.
3. Add the water and cover with a lid. Adjust to low heat and let it cook for 10 minutes. Serve with white rice.

Per serving: Calories: 31kcal; Fat: 0.23oz; Carbs: 0.26oz; Protein: 0.074oz; Sodium: 39.3mg; Potassium: 0.0074oz; Phosphorus: 0.0015oz

222. Baked Tofu with Steamed Broccoli

Preparation time: 10 minutes

Cooking time: 25 minutes

Servings: 4

Ingredients:

- 1 block extra-firm tofu, pressed then cut into cubes
- 2 tablespoons low-sodium soy sauce
- 1 tablespoon maple syrup
- 1 tablespoon rice vinegar
- 1 teaspoon sesame oil
- 4 cups broccoli florets
- 1 tablespoon sesame seeds (optional)

Directions:

1. Preheat the oven to 400 deg. F. Line a baking sheet with parchment paper.
2. In your bowl, whisk together the soy sauce, maple syrup, rice vinegar, and sesame oil.
3. Place the tofu cubes on the prepared baking sheet and pour the marinade over them. Toss to coat evenly.
4. Bake the tofu for 20-25 minutes, or until crispy.
5. Meanwhile, steam the broccoli until tender.
6. Serve the baked tofu with steamed broccoli and sprinkle with sesame seeds if desired.

Per serving: Calories: 180kcal; Fat: 0.28oz; Carbs: 0.49oz; Protein: 0.49oz; Sodium: 220mg; Potassium: 0.0106oz; Phosphorus: 0.0071oz

223. Zucchini Noodles with Tomato-Basil Sauce

Preparation time: 15 minutes

Cooking time: 15 minutes

Servings: 2

Ingredients:

- 2 large zucchini, spiralized
- 2 cups cherry tomatoes, halved
- 2 cloves garlic, minced
- 1 tablespoon olive oil
- 1/4 cup fresh basil, chopped
- Salt and pepper to taste

Directions:

1. In a huge pan, heat the olive oil over medium heat. Add the garlic and sauté until fragrant.
2. Place the cherry tomatoes to the pan then cook for about 5 minutes, 'til they start to soften and release their juices.
3. Season with salt and pepper to taste.
4. Add the zucchini noodles to the pan then cook for an additional 3-4 minutes, 'til tender.
5. Remove from heat then stir in the fresh basil.

6. Serve immediately.

Per serving: Calories: 120kcal; Fat: 0.25oz; Carbs: 0.46oz; Protein: 0.14oz; Sodium: 30mg; Potassium: 0.0124oz; Phosphorus: 0.0035oz

224. Vegan Roasted Brussels Sprouts

Preparation time: 10 minutes

Cooking time: 30 minutes

Servings: 4

Ingredients:

- 1 lb Brussels sprouts, trimmed and halved
- 2 tablespoons olive oil
- 2 cloves garlic, minced
- 1 teaspoon dried thyme
- Salt and pepper to taste

Directions:

1. Preheat the oven to 400 deg. F. Line a baking sheet with parchment paper.
2. In a huge bowl, combine the Brussels sprouts, olive oil, garlic, dried thyme, salt, and pepper. Toss until the Brussels sprouts are coated.
3. Transfer the Brussels sprouts in a single layer on the prepared baking sheet.
4. Roast in preheated oven for about 25-30 mins, or 'til the Brussels sprouts are tender and slightly caramelized, stirring halfway through.
5. Serve hot.

Per serving: Calories: 120kcal; Fat: 0.25oz; Carbs: 0.42oz; Protein: 0.14oz; Sodium: 20mg; Potassium: 0.0106oz; Phosphorus: 0.0028oz

225. Lentil and Vegetable Soup

Preparation time: 10 minutes

Cooking time: 30 minutes

Servings: 6

Ingredients:

- 1 cup green lentils, rinsed
- 1 onion, diced
- 2 carrots, diced
- 2 celery stalks, diced
- 2 cloves garlic, minced
- 4 cups low-sodium vegetable broth
- 2 cups water

- 1 teaspoon dried thyme
- 1 bay leaf
- Salt and pepper to taste

Directions:

1. In a large pot, sauté the onion, carrots, celery, and garlic over medium heat until softened.
2. Add the lentils, vegetable broth, water, thyme, bay leaf, salt, and pepper to the pot.
3. Boil the mixture, then reduce heat then simmer for about 30 minutes or until the lentils are tender.
4. Remove the bay leaf before serving.

Per serving: Calories: 180kcal; Fat: 0.018oz; Carbs: 1.16oz; Protein: 0.42oz; Sodium: 120mg; Potassium: 0.0106oz; Phosphorus: 0.0071oz

226. Quinoa-Stuffed Bell Peppers

Preparation time: 20 minutes

Cooking time: 45 minutes

Servings: 4

Ingredients:

- 4 bell peppers (any color), tops removed and seeds removed
- 1 cup cooked quinoa
- 1 can black beans, rinsed and drained
- 1 cup corn kernels
- 1/2 cup diced tomatoes
- 1/4 cup chopped cilantro
- 1 teaspoon ground cumin
- 1/2 teaspoon chili powder
- Salt and pepper to taste

Directions:

1. Preheat the oven to 375 deg. F. Bring the bell peppers in a baking dish.
2. In a huge bowl, combine the cooked quinoa, black beans, corn kernels, diced tomatoes, cilantro, cumin, chili powder, salt, and pepper.
3. Spoon the quinoa mixture into each bell pepper, filling them to the top.
4. Cover the baking dish with foil then bake for 35-40 minutes, or 'til the peppers are tender.
5. Take the foil then bake for an additional 5 minutes to lightly brown the tops.
6. Serve hot.

Per serving: Calories: 230kcal; Fat: 0.035oz; Carbs: 1.62oz; Protein: 0.42oz; Sodium: 60mg; Potassium: 0.0106oz; Phosphorus: 0.0071oz

227. Quinoa Salad with Lemon-Dijon Dressing

Preparation time: 15 minutes

Cooking time: 20 minutes

Servings: 4

Ingredients:

- 1 cup cooked quinoa
- 1 cup cucumber, diced
- 1 cup cherry tomatoes, halved
- 1/4 cup red onion, finely chopped
- 2 tablespoons fresh parsley, chopped
- 2 tablespoons fresh lemon juice
- 1 tablespoon Dijon mustard
- 1 tablespoon olive oil
- Salt and pepper to taste

Directions:

1. In a huge bowl, combine the cooked quinoa, cucumber, cherry tomatoes, red onion, and parsley.
2. In a separate small bowl, whisk together the lemon juice, Dijon mustard, olive oil, salt, and pepper.
3. Transfer the dressing over the quinoa mixture then toss to combine. Adjust seasoning if needed.
4. Serve chilled or at room temperature.

Per serving: Calories: 180kcal; Fat: 0.18oz; Carbs: 0.99oz; Protein: 0.21oz; Sodium: 80mg; Potassium: 0.0081oz; Phosphorus: 0.0035oz

228. Vegan Tomato and Basil Pasta

Preparation time: 10 minutes

Cooking time: 20 minutes

Servings: 4

Ingredients:

- 8 oz whole wheat or gluten-free pasta
- 2 tablespoons olive oil
- 1 onion, diced
- 2 cloves garlic, minced
- 1 can diced tomatoes
- 1/4 cup tomato paste
- 1/4 cup chopped fresh basil
- 1/2 teaspoon dried oregano
- Salt and pepper to taste

Directions:

1. Cook the pasta according to package instructions. Drain and set aside.
2. In your huge skillet, heat the olive oil over medium heat. Add the onion and garlic. Sauté until the onion is translucent.
3. Add the diced tomatoes, tomato paste, basil, oregano, salt, and pepper to the skillet. Stir to combine.
4. Simmer the sauce for about 10 minutes to allow the flavors to meld together.
5. Place the cooked pasta to the skillet then toss to coat the pasta with the sauce.
6. Serve hot.

Per serving: Calories: 280kcal; Fat: 0.25oz; Carbs: 1.69oz; Protein: 0.35oz; Sodium: 230mg; Potassium: 0.0106oz; Phosphorus: 0.0053oz

229. Cauliflower Rice Stir-Fry

Preparation time: 15 minutes

Cooking time: 15 minutes

Servings: 4

Ingredients:

- 1 small head cauliflower
- 1 tablespoon vegetable oil
- 1 onion, diced
- 2 cloves garlic, minced
- 1 carrot, diced
- 1 cup frozen peas
- 2 tablespoons low-sodium soy sauce
- 1 tablespoon sesame oil
- Salt and pepper to taste

Directions:

1. Cut the cauliflower into florets, then place them in a food processor. Pulse until the cauliflower resembles rice.
2. Heat the vegetable oil in a huge skillet or wok over medium heat. Add the onion, garlic, and carrot. Sauté until the vegetables are tender.
3. Add the cauliflower rice and frozen peas to the skillet. Cook for about 5-7 minutes, stirring occasionally, 'til the cauliflower is tender.

4. Stir in the soy sauce & sesame oil. Season with salt and pepper to taste.
5. Cook for 2-3 minutes to heat through.
6. Serve hot.

Per serving: Calories: 110kcal; Fat: 0.21oz; Carbs: 0.42oz; Protein: 0.14oz; Sodium: 240mg; Potassium: 0.0124oz; Phosphorus: 0.0035oz

230. Vegan Lentil Loaf

Preparation time: 15 minutes

Cooking time: 1 hour

Servings: 6

Ingredients:

- 1 cup green lentils, rinsed
- 1 onion, diced
- 2 cloves garlic, minced
- 1 carrot, grated
- 1 stalk celery, diced
- 1 bell pepper, diced
- 1/4 cup tomato paste
- 1 tablespoon low-sodium soy sauce
- 1 tablespoon ground flaxseed mixed + 3 tablespoons water (flax egg)
- 1 tablespoon chopped fresh parsley
- 1 teaspoon dried thyme
- 1 teaspoon dried oregano
- 1/2 teaspoon paprika
- Salt and pepper to taste

Directions:

1. Preheat the oven to 375 deg. F. Grease a loaf pan or line it with parchment paper.
2. Cook the lentils according to package instructions 'til tender. Drain any excess water and set aside.
3. In a skillet, sauté the onion, garlic, carrot, celery, and bell pepper until the vegetables are tender.
4. In a huge bowl, combine the cooked lentils, sautéed vegetables, tomato paste, soy sauce, flax egg, parsley, thyme, oregano, paprika, salt, and pepper. Mix well.
5. Transfer the lentil mixture to the prepared loaf pan. Press it down firmly.
6. Bake for 45-50 minutes, or until the loaf is firm and slightly browned on top.
7. Allow the loaf to cool for a few minutes before slicing.

8. Serve warm.

Per serving: Calories: 190kcal; Fat: 0.035oz; Carbs: 1.27oz; Protein: 0.39oz; Sodium: 120mg; Potassium: 0.0141oz; Phosphorus: 0.0071oz

231. Vegan Cabbage Stir-Fry

Preparation time: 10 minutes

Cooking time: 15 minutes

Servings: 4

Ingredients:

- 1 small head cabbage, shredded
- 1 onion, thinly sliced
- 2 cloves garlic, minced
- 1 carrot, julienned
- 1 red bell pepper, thinly sliced
- 2 tablespoons low-sodium soy sauce
- 1 tablespoon rice vinegar
- 1 teaspoon sesame oil
- 1/2 teaspoon ground ginger
- Salt and pepper to taste
- Sesame seeds (for garnish)

Directions:

1. In a large skillet or wok, heat a small amount of water over medium-high heat. Add the onion and garlic. Sauté until fragrant and the onion begins to soften.
2. Add the shredded cabbage, carrot, and bell pepper to the skillet. Stir-fry for about 5-7 minutes, or until the vegetables are tender-crisp.
3. In your small bowl, whisk together the soy sauce, rice vinegar, sesame oil, ground ginger, salt, and pepper.
4. Pour the sauce over the cabbage mixture. Stir-fry for an additional 2-3 minutes to coat the vegetables then allow the flavors to meld.
5. Garnish with sesame seeds before serving.
6. Serve hot.

Per serving: Calories: 100kcal; Fat: 0.071oz; Carbs: 0.64oz; Protein: 0.18oz; Sodium: 150mg; Potassium: 0.0124oz; Phosphorus: 0.0028oz

232. Black Bean and Sweet Potato Tacos

Preparation time: 15 minutes

Cooking time: 30 minutes

Servings: 4

Ingredients:

- 1 tablespoon vegetable oil
- 1 onion, diced
- 2 cloves garlic, minced
- 1 sweet potato, peeled and diced
- 1 can black beans, rinsed and drained
- 1 teaspoon ground cumin
- 1/2 teaspoon chili powder
- 1/2 teaspoon paprika
- Salt and pepper to taste
- 8 small corn tortillas
- Toppings: sliced avocado, chopped fresh cilantro, salsa (optional)

Directions:

1. In your skillet, heat the vegetable oil over medium heat. Add the onion and garlic. Sauté until the onion is translucent.
2. Place the diced sweet potato to the skillet. Cook for about 10-12 minutes, or until the sweet potato is tender.
3. Add the black beans, cumin, chili powder, paprika, salt, and pepper to the skillet. Stir to combine then cook for 5 mins to heat through.
4. Warm the corn tortillas in a separate skillet or oven.
5. Fill each tortilla with the black bean and sweet potato mixture.
6. Top with sliced avocado, chopped cilantro, and salsa if desired.
7. Serve warm.

Per serving: Calories: 240kcal; Fat: 0.21oz; Carbs: 1.44oz; Protein: 0.28oz; Sodium: 120mg; Potassium: 0.0124oz; Phosphorus: 0.0053oz

233. Vegan Tofu Stir-Fry

Preparation time: 15 minutes

Cooking time: 20 minutes

Servings: 4

Ingredients:

- 1 block extra-firm tofu, drained and cubed
- 2 tablespoons low-sodium soy sauce
- 1 tablespoon cornstarch
- 1 tablespoon vegetable oil

- 1 bell pepper, thinly sliced
- 1 carrot, thinly sliced
- 1 cup broccoli florets
- 1 cup snow peas
- 2 cloves garlic, minced
- 1 tablespoon grated fresh ginger
- 2 tablespoons low-sodium soy sauce
- 1 tablespoon rice vinegar
- 1 teaspoon sesame oil
- Salt and pepper to taste
- Green onions, chopped (for garnish)

Directions:

1. In a shallow dish, combine the tofu, soy sauce, and cornstarch. Toss until the tofu is coated. Set aside for 10 minutes.
2. In a large skillet or wok, heat the vegetable oil over medium-high heat. Add the tofu and cook for about 5-7 minutes, or until golden brown and crispy. Remove the tofu from the skillet then set aside.
3. In your same skillet, add the bell pepper, carrot, broccoli, snow peas, garlic, and ginger. Stir-fry for about 5 minutes, or 'til the vegetables are tender-crisp.
4. In your small bowl, whisk together the soy sauce, rice vinegar, sesame oil, salt & pepper.
5. Return the tofu to the skillet then pour the sauce over the tofu and vegetables. Stir-fry for an additional 2-3 minutes to coat everything and heat through.
6. Garnish with chopped green onions before serving.
7. Serve hot.

Per serving: Calories: 200kcal; Fat: 0.35oz; Carbs: 0.53oz; Protein: 0.53oz; Sodium: 350mg; Potassium: 0.0106oz; Phosphorus: 0.0078oz

234. Vegan Lentil Chili

Preparation time: 10 minutes

Cooking time: 40 minutes

Servings: 6

Ingredients:

- 1 cup green lentils, rinsed
- 1 onion, diced
- 2 cloves garlic, minced

- 1 bell pepper, diced
- 1 can diced tomatoes
- 1 can tomato sauce
- 2 cups low-sodium vegetable broth
- 2 teaspoons chili powder
- 1 teaspoon cumin
- 1/2 teaspoon paprika
- Salt and pepper to taste

Directions:

1. In a large pot, sauté the onion, garlic, and bell pepper over medium heat 'til softened.
2. Add the lentils, diced tomatoes, tomato sauce, vegetable broth, chili powder, cumin, paprika, salt, and pepper to the pot.
3. Boil the mixture, then reduce heat and simmer for about 30-35 minutes, or until the lentils are tender.
4. Adjust seasoning if needed.
5. Serve hot.

Per serving: Calories: 200kcal; Fat: 0.035oz; Carbs: 1.34oz; Protein: 0.42oz; Sodium: 200mg; Potassium: 0.0106oz; Phosphorus: 0.0071oz

235. Quinoa and Vegetable Stir-Fry

Preparation time: 10 minutes

Cooking time: 20 minutes

Servings: 4

Ingredients:

- 1 cup cooked quinoa
- 1 tablespoon vegetable oil
- 1 onion, sliced
- 2 cloves garlic, minced
- 1 bell pepper, sliced
- 1 zucchini, sliced
- 1 cup sliced mushrooms
- 2 cups broccoli florets
- 2 tablespoons low-sodium soy sauce
- 1 tablespoon rice vinegar
- 1 tablespoon maple syrup
- Salt and pepper to taste

Directions:

1. In a huge skillet or wok, heat the vegetable oil over medium-high heat. Add the onion and garlic.

Sauté until fragrant and the onion begins to soften.

2. Add the bell pepper, zucchini, mushrooms, and broccoli to the skillet. Stir-fry for about 5-7 minutes, or until the vegetables are tender-crisp.
3. In your small bowl, whisk together the soy sauce, rice vinegar, maple syrup, salt, and pepper.
4. Push the vegetables to one side of the skillet. Add the cooked quinoa to the other side and pour the sauce over the quinoa.
5. Stir-fry for an additional 2-3 minutes to heat through and allow the flavors to blend.
6. Serve hot.

Per serving: Calories: 200kcal; Fat: 0.14oz; Carbs: 1.31oz; Protein: 0.25oz; Sodium: 270mg; Potassium: 0.1209oz; Phosphorus: 0.0053oz

236. Vegan Spinach and Mushroom Pasta

Preparation time: 10 minutes

Cooking time: 20 minutes

Servings: 4

Ingredients:

- 8 oz whole wheat or gluten-free pasta
- 1 tablespoon olive oil
- 1 onion, diced
- 2 cloves garlic, minced
- 8 oz mushrooms, sliced
- 4 cups fresh spinach leaves
- 1/4 cup vegetable broth
- 1/4 cup nutritional yeast (optional)
- Salt and pepper to taste

Directions:

1. Cook the pasta according to package instructions. Drain and set aside.
2. In your huge skillet, heat the olive oil over medium heat. Add the onion and garlic. Sauté until the onion is translucent.
3. Add the mushrooms to the skillet. Cook for about 5 minutes, or until the mushrooms are tender and browned.
4. Add the spinach and vegetable broth to the skillet. Cook for 2-3 minutes, or until the spinach has wilted.
5. Add the cooked pasta to the skillet. Toss to combine.

6. Stir in the nutritional yeast, if using. Season with salt and pepper.

7. Serve hot.

Per serving: Calories: 280kcal; Fat: 0.14oz; Carbs: 1.83oz; Protein: 0.49oz; Sodium: 220mg; Potassium: 0.0127oz; Phosphorus: 0.0053oz

237. Roasted Cauliflower and Chickpea Salad

Preparation time: 15 minutes

Cooking time: 25 minutes

Servings: 4

Ingredients:

- 1 head cauliflower, cut into florets
- 1 can chickpeas, rinsed and drained
- 2 tablespoons olive oil
- 1 teaspoon ground cumin
- 1 teaspoon paprika
- 1/2 teaspoon turmeric
- Juice of 1 lemon
- 2 cups mixed salad greens
- Salt and pepper to taste

Directions:

1. Preheat the oven to 425 deg. F. Line a baking sheet with parchment paper.

2. In a huge bowl, combine the cauliflower florets, chickpeas, olive oil, cumin, paprika, turmeric, salt, and pepper. Toss to coat evenly.

3. Spread the cauliflower and chickpeas on the prepared baking sheet then roast for 20-25 mins, or 'til golden brown.

4. In a different bowl, whisk together the lemon juice, olive oil, salt & pepper to make the dressing.

5. Arrange the mixed salad greens on a serving plate then top with the roasted cauliflower and chickpeas.

6. Transfer the dressing over the salad then serve.

Per serving: Calories: 180kcal; Fat: 0.28oz; Carbs: 0.99oz; Protein: 0.25oz; Sodium: 100mg; Potassium: 0.0124oz; Phosphorus: 0.0053oz

238. Vegan Chickpea Curry

Preparation time: 15 minutes

Cooking time: 30 minutes

Servings: 4

Ingredients:

- 1 tablespoon vegetable oil
- 1 onion, diced
- 2 cloves garlic, minced
- 1 bell pepper, diced
- 1 carrot, diced
- 1 can chickpeas, rinsed and drained
- 1 can coconut milk
- 2 tablespoons curry powder
- 1 teaspoon ground cumin
- 1/2 teaspoon turmeric
- Salt and pepper to taste

Directions:

1. In a huge pot or skillet, heat the vegetable oil over medium heat. Add the onion and garlic. Sauté until the onion is translucent.

2. Add the bell pepper and carrot to the pot. Cook for about 5 minutes, or until the vegetables begin to soften.

3. Add the chickpeas, coconut milk, curry powder, cumin, turmeric, salt, and pepper to the pot. Stir to combine.

4. Simmer the curry for about 20 minutes, stirring occasionally, to allow the flavors to develop.

5. Serve hot with rice or naan bread.

Per serving: Calories: 320kcal; Fat: 0.53oz; Carbs: 1.41oz; Protein: 0.35oz; Sodium: 200mg; Potassium: 0.1137oz; Phosphorus: 0.0053oz

239. Vegan Ratatouille

Preparation time: 20 minutes

Cooking time: 40 minutes

Servings: 4

Ingredients:

- 2 tablespoons olive oil
- 1 onion, diced
- 2 cloves garlic, minced
- 1 eggplant, diced
- 1 zucchini, diced
- 1 bell pepper, diced
- 1 can diced tomatoes
- 1 teaspoon dried thyme
- 1 teaspoon dried oregano
- Salt and pepper to taste

- Fresh basil, chopped (for garnish)

Directions:

1. In a huge pot or skillet, heat the olive oil over medium heat. Add the onion and garlic. Sauté until the onion is translucent.

2. Add the diced eggplant, zucchini, bell pepper, diced tomatoes (with their juices), thyme, oregano, salt, and pepper to the pot. Stir to combine.

3. Simmer the ratatouille for about 30-40 minutes, stirring occasionally, 'til the vegetables are tender and the flavors have melded together.

4. Garnish with fresh basil before serving.

5. Serve hot.

Per serving: Calories: 160kcal; Fat: 0.25oz; Carbs: 0.78oz; Protein: 0.14oz; Sodium: 190mg; Potassium: 0.1367oz; Phosphorus: 0.0035oz

240. Vegan Stuffed Bell Peppers

Preparation time: 20 minutes

Cooking time: 45 minutes

Servings: 4

Ingredients:

- 4 bell peppers (any color), tops removed and seeded
- 1 cup cooked quinoa
- 1 can black beans, rinsed and drained
- 1/2 cup corn kernels
- 1/2 cup diced tomatoes
- 1/4 cup chopped fresh cilantro
- 1 teaspoon ground cumin
- 1/2 teaspoon chili powder
- Salt and pepper to taste

Directions:

1. Preheat the oven to 375 deg. F. Grease a baking dish.

2. In a huge bowl, combine the cooked quinoa, black beans, corn kernels, diced tomatoes, cilantro, cumin, chili powder, salt, and pepper. Mix well.

3. Stuff each bell pepper with the quinoa and bean mixture.

4. Place the stuffed bell peppers in the baking dish.

5. Bake for 40-45 minutes, or 'til the peppers are tender and slightly charred.

6. Serve hot.

Per serving: Calories: 250kcal; Fat: 0.071oz; Carbs: 1.76oz; Protein: 0.42oz; Sodium: 180mg; Potassium: 0.1286oz; Phosphorus: 0.0071oz

Chapter 13.   Vegan Dessert Recipes

241. Baked Peach Crumble

Preparation time: 15 minutes
Cooking time: 30 minutes
Servings: 6
Ingredients:

- 4 cups sliced peaches (fresh or frozen)
- 2 tablespoons lemon juice
- 1/2 cup rolled oats
- 1/4 cup almond flour
- 2 tablespoons coconut oil
- 2 tablespoons sugar substitute (check for phosphorus content)
- 1/2 teaspoon cinnamon
- Pinch of salt

Directions:

1. Preheat the oven to 350 deg. F.
2. In a bowl, toss the peaches with lemon juice.
3. Spread the peaches in a baking dish.
4. In a different bowl, combine the oats, almond flour, coconut oil, sugar substitute, cinnamon, and salt. Mix until crumbly.
5. Sprinkle the crumble mixture equally over the peaches.
6. Bake for 30 minutes or 'til the topping is golden brown & the peaches are tender.
7. Let the crumble to cool slightly before serving.

Per serving: Calories: 150kcal; Fat: 0.25oz; Carbs: 0.78oz; Protein: 0.071oz; Sodium: 0mg; Potassium: 0.0095oz; Phosphorus: 0.0014oz

242. Coconut Raspberry Popsicles

Preparation time: 5 minutes (plus freezing time)
Cooking time: 0 minutes
Servings: 4
Ingredients:

- 1 cup canned coconut milk (light)
- 1/2 cup fresh or frozen raspberries
- 1 tablespoon sugar substitute (check for phosphorus content)
- 1/2 teaspoon vanilla extract

Directions:

1. In a blender, combine the coconut milk, raspberries, sugar substitute, and vanilla extract.
2. Blend until smooth.
3. Pour the mixture into popsicle molds then insert popsicle sticks.
4. Freeze for at least 4 hours or until solid.
5. To take the popsicles from the molds, briefly run warm water over the molds and gently pull the popsicles out.
6. Serve immediately.

Per serving: Calories: 90kcal; Fat: 0.28oz; Carbs: 0.14oz; Protein: 0.035oz; Sodium: 15mg; Potassium: 0.0039oz; Phosphorus: 0.0011oz

243. Chocolate Avocado Mousse

Preparation time: 10 minutes
Cooking time: 0 minutes
Servings: 4
Ingredients:

- 2 ripe avocados
- 1/4 cup unsweetened cocoa powder
- 1/4 cup sugar substitute (check for phosphorus content)
- 1/4 cup almond milk
- 1/2 teaspoon vanilla extract
- Pinch of salt

Directions:

1. Scoop out the flesh of the avocados and place them in a blender or food processor.
2. Add the cocoa powder, sugar substitute, almond milk, vanilla extract, and salt.
3. Blend 'til smooth and creamy, scraping down the sides as needed.
4. Divide the mousse into serving bowls or glasses.
5. Refrigerate for 1 hour before serving.

Per serving: Calories: 150kcal; Fat: 0.35oz; Carbs: 0.53oz; Protein: 0.071oz; Sodium: 0mg; Potassium: 0.0152oz; Phosphorus: 0.0025oz

244. Baked Apples with Cinnamon

Preparation time: 10 minutes

Cooking time: 40 minutes

Servings: 4

Ingredients:

- 4 medium-sized apples
- 1 tablespoon cinnamon
- 1 tablespoon sugar substitute (check for phosphorus content)
- 1/4 cup water

Directions:

1. Preheat the oven to 350 deg. F.
2. Core the apples then place them in a baking dish.
3. In your small bowl, mix together the cinnamon and sugar substitute.
4. Sprinkle the cinnamon mixture over the apples.
5. Pour the water into the baking dish.
6. Bake the apples for 40 minutes or until they are tender.
7. Serve warm.

Per serving: Calories: 100kcal; Fat: 0oz; Carbs: 0.95oz; Protein: 0oz; Sodium: 0mg; Potassium: 0.0069oz; Phosphorus: 0.0004oz

245. Oatmeal Raisin Cookies

Preparation time: 15 minutes

Cooking time: 12 minutes

Servings: 12

Ingredients:

- 1 cup rolled oats
- 1/2 cup almond flour
- 1/4 cup raisins
- 1/4 cup unsweetened applesauce
- 2 tablespoons maple syrup
- 1/2 teaspoon cinnamon
- 1/2 teaspoon vanilla extract

Directions:

1. Preheat the oven to 350 deg. F.

2. In your bowl, combine the oats, almond flour, raisins, applesauce, maple syrup, cinnamon, and vanilla extract.
3. Stir until well combined.
4. Drop spoonfuls of the cookie dough in a baking sheet lined with parchment paper.
5. Flatten all cookie slightly with the back of a spoon.
6. Bake for 12 minutes or until golden brown around the edges.
7. Let the cookies to cool on the baking sheet for a few minutes, then place them to a wire rack to cool completely.

Per serving: Calories: 90kcal; Fat: 0.11oz; Carbs: 0.53oz; Protein: 0.071oz; Sodium: 0mg; Potassium: 0.0032oz; Phosphorus: 0.0021oz

246. Peanut Butter Energy Balls

Preparation time: 15 minutes

Cooking time: 0 minutes

Servings: 12

Ingredients:

- 1 cup rolled oats
- 1/2 cup natural peanut butter (low sodium)
- 1/4 cup ground flaxseed
- 1/4 cup unsweetened shredded coconut
- 2 tablespoons maple syrup
- 1/2 teaspoon vanilla extract

Directions:

1. In a bowl, combine the rolled oats, peanut butter, ground flaxseed, shredded coconut, maple syrup, and vanilla extract.
2. Stir until well combined.
3. Roll the mixture in a small balls, about 1 inch in diameter.
4. Place the energy balls on a baking sheet lined with parchment paper.
5. Refrigerate for 1 hour to firm up.
6. Place in an airtight container in the refrigerator.

Per serving: Calories: 110kcal; Fat: 0.25oz; Carbs: 0.32oz; Protein: 0.11oz; Sodium: 45mg; Potassium: 0.0034oz; Phosphorus: 0.0023oz

247. Watermelon Lime Sorbet

Preparation time: 10 minutes (plus freezing time)

Cooking time: 0 minutes

Servings: 6

Ingredients:

- 4 cups cubed seedless watermelon
- 2 tablespoons lime juice
- 1 tablespoon sugar substitute (check for phosphorus content)
- Fresh mint leaves for garnish (optional)

Directions:

1. Bring the watermelon cubes in a blender and blend until smooth.
2. Add the lime juice and sugar substitute, and blend again until well combined.
3. Transfer the mixture into a shallow dish or ice cream maker and freeze.
4. Every 30 minutes, take the dish from the freezer then scrape the mixture with a fork to break up any ice crystals. Repeat this process 3-4 times until the sorbet reaches the desired consistency.
5. Serve the sorbet in bowls, garnished with fresh mint leaves if desired.

Per serving: Calories: 40kcal; Fat: 0oz; Carbs: 0.35oz; Protein: 0.035oz; Sodium: 0mg; Potassium: 0.0042oz; Phosphorus: 0.0004oz

248. Vanilla Bean Panna Cotta

Preparation time: 10 minutes (plus chilling time)

Cooking time: 5 minutes

Servings: 4

Ingredients:

- 1 1/2 cups unsweetened almond milk
- 1/4 cup sugar substitute (check for phosphorus content)
- 1 teaspoon vanilla extract
- 1 tablespoon agar agar flakes (vegetable-based gelatin)
- Fresh berries for topping (optional)

Directions:

1. In your saucepan, combine the almond milk, sugar substitute, vanilla extract, and agar agar flakes.
2. Place the mixture to a simmer in a medium heat, stirring occasionally.
3. Reduce the heat to low and let it simmer for 5 minutes, stirring continuously.

4. Remove from heat and let it cool for a few minutes.
5. Transfer the mixture into individual serving glasses or ramekins.
6. Refrigerate for at least 2 hours or until set.
7. Top with fresh berries before serving if desired.

Per serving: Calories: 40kcal; Fat: 0.035oz; Carbs: 0.28oz; Protein: 0.035oz; Sodium: 100mg; Potassium: 0.0014oz; Phosphorus: 0.0004oz

249. Vegan Chocolate Chip Cookies

Preparation time: 10 minutes

Cooking time: 12 minutes

Servings: 12

Ingredients:

- 1 1/2 cups oat flour (grind rolled oats in a blender)
- 1/2 cup almond flour
- 1/4 cup sugar substitute (check for phosphorus content)
- 1/4 cup coconut oil, melted
- 3 tablespoons unsweetened almond milk
- 2 tablespoons maple syrup
- 1/2 teaspoon vanilla extract
- 1/2 teaspoon baking powder
- 1/4 teaspoon salt
- 1/4 cup vegan chocolate chips

Directions:

1. Preheat the oven to 350 deg. F. Line a baking sheet with parchment paper.
2. In your bowl, combine the oat flour, almond flour, sugar substitute, coconut oil, almond milk, maple syrup, vanilla extract, baking powder, and salt. Stir until well combined.
3. Fold in the chocolate chips.
4. Drop spoonfuls of cookie dough in a prepared baking sheet, spacing them apart.
5. Flatten all cookie slightly with the back of a spoon.
6. Bake for 12 minutes or until golden brown around the edges.
7. Let the cookies to cool on a baking sheet for a few minutes, then bring them to a wire rack to cool completely.

Per serving: Calories: 140kcal; Fat: 0.32oz; Carbs: 0.46oz; Protein: 0.11oz; Sodium: 60mg; Potassium: 0.0032oz; Phosphorus: 0.0025oz

250. Mixed Fruit Salad with Mint-Lime Dressing

Preparation time: 10 minutes

Cooking time: 0 minutes

Servings: 4

Ingredients:

- 2 cups mixed fresh fruits (e.g., melon, berries, pineapple, kiwi)
- 2 tablespoons freshly squeezed lime juice
- 1 tablespoon sugar substitute (check for phosphorus content)
- 1 tablespoon chopped fresh mint leaves

Directions:

1. In a bowl, combine the mixed fresh fruits.
2. In a separate small bowl, whisk together the lime juice, sugar substitute, and chopped mint leaves.
3. Transfer the dressing over the fruit salad then toss gently to combine.
4. Serve chilled.

Per serving: Calories: 50kcal; Fat: 0oz; Carbs: 0.46oz; Protein: 0.035oz; Sodium: 0mg; Potassium: 0.0042oz; Phosphorus: 0.0004oz

60-Day Meal Plan

Day	Breakfast	Lunch	Dinner	Dessert
1	Breakfast Tacos	Curried Chicken with Cauliflower	Spiced Honey Salmon	Chocolate Muffins
2	Vegan Blueberry Muffins	Lentil and Vegetable Soup	Roasted Chicken Breast	Fruit Salad
3	Vegan Tofu Breakfast Burrito Bowl	Vegan Tomato and Basil Pasta	Chicken Breast and Bok Choy	Small Chocolate Cakes
4	Vegan Chia Pudding	Quinoa-Stuffed Bell Peppers	Ground Chicken with Basil	Frozen Fantasy
5	Buckwheat Pancakes	Vegan Lentil Loaf	Herby Beef Stroganoff and Fluffy Rice	Watermelon Lime Sorbet
6	Vegan Sweet Potato Breakfast Bowl	Vegan Lentil Chili	Herb-Roasted Lamb Chops	Oatmeal Raisin Cookies
7	Vegan Tofu Scramble Breakfast Tacos	Cauliflower Rice Stir-Fry	Beef Brisket	Coconut Raspberry Popsicles
8	Strawberry Muesli	Quinoa Salad with Lemon-Dijon Dressing	Pork Loins with Leeks	Baked Peach Crumble
9	Italian Breakfast Frittata	Vegan Cabbage Stir-Fry	Teriyaki Beef Skewers	Peanut Butter Energy Balls
10	Vegan Tofu Benedict	Black Bean and Sweet Potato Tacos	Pork Tenderloin with Roasted Fruit	Mixed Fruit Salad with Mint-Lime Dressing
11	Pineapple Bread	Vegan Lentil Curry	Chicken Egg Breakfast Muffins	Vanilla Bean Panna Cotta
12	Vegan Breakfast Quinoa Bars	Vegan Tofu Stir-Fry	Beef Stir-Fry	Chocolate Avocado Mousse
13	Omelet with Feta and Fresh Mint	Roasted Cauliflower and Chickpea Salad	Grilled Lemony Cod	Baked Apples with Cinnamon
14	Yogurt Bulgur	Vegan Ratatouille	Peppercorn Pork Chops	Vegan Chocolate Chip Cookies
15	Vegan Zucchini Fritters	Vegan Chickpea Curry	Quinoa and Vegetable Stir-Fry	Mixed Berry Cobbler
16	Apple Omelet	Vegan Stuffed Bell Peppers	Beer Pork Ribs	Strawberry Tiramisu
17	Vegan Overnight Oats	Vegan Spinach and Mushroom Pasta	Open-Faced Beef Stir-Up	Fruit Crunch
18	Cauliflower & Pear Porridge	Haddock and Oiled Leeks	Salmon Baked in Foil with Fresh Thyme	Frozen Lemon Dessert

19	Whole Grain Pancakes	Broiled Shrimp	Baked Fennel and Garlic Sea Bass	Chocolate Beet Cake
20	Vegan Tofu and Vegetable Stir-Fry	Poached Halibut in Mango Sauce	Sardine Fish Cakes	Sandy Cake
21	Easy Turnip Puree	Grilled Chicken	Chili Mussels	Strawberry Pie
22	Crunchy Granola Yogurt Bowl	Saucy Fish Dill	Shrimp in Garlic Sauce	Sweet Raspberry Candy
23	Celery and Kale Mix	Broiled Salmon Fillets	Citrus Glazed Salmon	Pineapple Cake
24	Vegan Breakfast Couscous	Herbed Vegetable Trout	Fish with Mushrooms	Blueberry Espresso Brownies
25	Vegan Breakfast Quinoa Salad	Oven-Fried Southern Style Catfish	Ground Chicken with Basil	Gumdrop Cookies
26	Egg and Avocado Bake	Sardine Fish Cakes	Roast Beef	Ribbon Cakes
27	Vegan Tofu Scramble	Citrus Glazed Salmon	Beef Brochettes	Spritz Cookies
28	Stuffed Sweet Potatoes	Spicy Lamb Curry	Grilled Pork Tenderloin	Jeweled Cookies
29	Vegan Tofu Breakfast Burrito	Baked Tofu with Steamed Broccoli	Chicken Breast and Bok Choy	Lemon Cake
30	Fruit Salad with Coconut Yogurt	Quinoa and Vegetable Stir-Fry	Roasted Chicken Breast	Watermelon Mint Granita
31	Vegan Breakfast Burrito	Lentil and Vegetable Soup	Grilled Chicken	Chocolate Muffins
32	Buckwheat Pancakes	Vegan Lentil Loaf	Teriyaki Beef Skewers	Fruit Salad
33	Veggie Scramble	Quinoa-Stuffed Bell Peppers	Creamy Turkey	Coconut Raspberry Popsicles
34	Spinach and Mushroom Frittata	Vegan Cabbage Stir-Fry	Ground Chicken with Basil	Baked Peach Crumble
35	Oatmeal with Apples and Cinnamon	Vegan Lentil Curry	Herb-Roasted Lamb Chops	Peanut Butter Energy Balls
36	Vegan Blueberry Muffins	Black Bean and Sweet Potato Tacos	Pork Tenderloin with Roasted Fruit	Mixed Fruit Salad with Mint-Lime Dressing
37	Breakfast Wrap with Fruit and Cheese	Vegan Ratatouille	Spiced Honey Salmon	Vanilla Bean Panna Cotta
38	Vegan Tofu Scramble Breakfast Tacos	Cauliflower Rice Stir-Fry	Beef Brisket	Chocolate Avocado Mousse
39	Strawberry Muesli	Quinoa Salad with Lemon-Dijon Dressing	Chicken Breast and Bok Choy	Baked Apples with Cinnamon
40	Vegan Tofu Benedict	Vegan Chickpea Curry	Roasted Chicken Breast	Vegan Chocolate Chip Cookies
41	Pineapple Bread	Vegan Spinach and Mushroom Pasta	Peppercorn Pork Chops	Mixed Berry Cobbler

42	Vegan Breakfast Quinoa Bars	Vegan Stuffed Bell Peppers	Beer Pork Ribs	Strawberry Tiramisu
43	Omelet with Feta and Fresh Mint	Roasted Cauliflower and Chickpea Salad	Herby Beef Stroganoff and Fluffy Rice	Fruit Crunch
44	Yogurt Bulgur	Vegan Tomato and Basil Pasta	Salmon Baked in Foil with Fresh Thyme	Frozen Lemon Dessert
45	Vegan Zucchini Fritters	Haddock and Oiled Leeks	Grilled Lemony Cod	Chocolate Beet Cake
46	Apple Omelet	Broiled Shrimp	Baked Fennel and Garlic Sea Bass	Sandy Cake
47	Vegan Overnight Oats	Poached Halibut in Mango Sauce	Sardine Fish Cakes	Blueberry Espresso Brownies
48	Cauliflower & Pear Porridge	Herbed Vegetable Trout	Ground Chicken with Basil	Gumdrop Cookies
49	Whole Grain Pancakes	Oven-Fried Southern Style Catfish	Beef Stir-Fry	Ribbon Cakes
50	Vegan Tofu and Vegetable Stir-Fry	Spicy Lamb Curry	Chicken Breast and Bok Choy	Spritz Cookies
51	Easy Turnip Puree	Baked Tofu with Steamed Broccoli	Roast Beef	Jeweled Cookies
52	Vegan Chia Pudding	Citrus Glazed Salmon	Beef Brochettes	Lemon Cake
53	Stuffed Sweet Potatoes	Vegan Lentil Chili	Grilled Pork Tenderloin	Watermelon Mint Granita
54	Veggie Breakfast Burrito	Lentil and Vegetable Soup	Herby Beef Stroganoff and Fluffy Rice	Chocolate Muffins
55	Blueberry Pancakes	Vegan Lentil Loaf	Teriyaki Beef Skewers	Fruit Salad
56	Avocado Toast with Eggs	Quinoa-Stuffed Bell Peppers	Creamy Turkey	Coconut Raspberry Popsicles
57	Veggie Omelet	Vegan Cabbage Stir-Fry	Ground Chicken with Basil	Baked Peach Crumble
58	Greek Yogurt with Berries	Vegan Lentil Curry	Herb-Roasted Lamb Chops	Peanut Butter Energy Balls
59	Banana Bread	Black Bean and Sweet Potato Tacos	Pork Tenderloin with Roasted Fruit	Mixed Fruit Salad with Mint-Lime Dressing
60	Breakfast Wrap with Avocado	Vegan Ratatouille	Spiced Honey Salmon	Vanilla Bean Panna Cotta

Measurement Conversion Chart

Volume Equivalents (Liquid)

US Standard	US Standard (ounces)	Metric (approximate)
2 tablespoons	1 fl. oz.	30 mL
¼ cup	2 fl. oz.	60 mL
½ cup	4 fl. oz.	120 mL
1 cup	8 fl. oz.	240 mL
1½ cups	12 fl. oz.	355 mL
2 cups or 1 pint	16 fl. oz.	475 mL
4 cups or 1 quart	32 fl. oz.	1 L
1 gallon	128 fl. oz.	4 L

Volume Equivalents (Dry)

US Standard	Metric (approximate)
⅛ teaspoon	0.5 mL
¼ teaspoon	1 mL
½ teaspoon	2 mL
¾ teaspoon	4 mL
1 teaspoon	5 mL
1 tablespoon	15 mL
¼ cup	59 mL
⅓ cup	79 mL
½ cup	118 mL
⅔ cup	156 mL
¾ cup	177 mL

1 cup	235 mL
2 cups or 1 pint	475 mL
3 cups	700 mL
4 cups or 1 quart	1 L

Oven Temperatures

Fahrenheit (F)	Celsius (C) (approximate)
250°F	120°C
300°F	150°C
325°F	165°C
350°F	180°C
375°F	190°C
400°F	200°C
425°F	220°C
450°F	230°C

Weight Equivalents

US Standard	Metric (approximate)
1 tablespoon	15 g
½ ounce	15 g
1 ounce	30 g
2 ounces	60 g
4 ounces	115 g
8 ounces	225 g
12 ounces	340 g
16 ounces or 1 pound	455 g

Conclusion

Nephropathy, or kidney disease, is a condition that requires careful attention to diet and nutrition. The right food choices can play a significant role in slowing down the progression of nephropathy and maintaining kidney health. By following a renal diet, individuals with nephropathy can optimize their nutritional intake while managing their kidney function.

A renal diet focuses on controlling key nutrients such as sodium, potassium, phosphorus, and protein to alleviate stress on the kidneys. It emphasizes lean sources of protein, low-potassium fruits and vegetables, limited phosphorus-rich foods, and reduced sodium intake. By making informed choices and being mindful of portion sizes, individuals can support their kidney function and overall well-being.

A renal diet is not about deprivation but rather about making conscious, flavorful choices that nourish the body while respecting the needs of the kidneys. It encourages creativity in the kitchen by exploring various herbs, spices, and other low-sodium seasonings to enhance the taste of meals. With the guidance of a registered dietitian, individuals can develop a personalized renal diet meal plan that suits their unique dietary needs and preferences.

By incorporating these principles into a renal diet, individuals with nephropathy and their families can discover a wealth of delicious and kidney-friendly recipes. This cookbook serves as a valuable resource, providing practical guidance, nutritional information, and flavorful recipes that make adhering to a renal diet an enjoyable and sustainable journey.

By embracing a renal diet and taking charge of their nutrition, individuals with nephropathy can take positive steps towards slowing down the progression of the disease, supporting their overall health, and improving their quality of life.

Index

Ground Chicken with Basil	50	Ribbon Cakes	79
Ground Turkey With Veggies	28	Roast Beef	56
Gumdrop Cookies	78	Roasted Cauliflower and Chickpea Salad	95
Haddock and Oiled Leeks	58	Roasted Chicken Breast	50
Hawaiian Chicken Salad	39	Roasted Mint Carrots	27
Herbed Cream Cheese Tartines	26	Roasted Peach Open-Face Sandwich	28
Herbed Vegetable Trout	60	Roasted Root Vegetables	67
Herb-Roasted Lamb Chops	54	Rosemary and White Bean Dip	71
Herby Beef Stroganoff and Fluffy Rice	50	Salmon And Green Beans	41
Honey Cinnamon Latte	20	Salmon and Pesto Salad	40
Hot Mulled Punch	19	Salmon Baked in Foil with Fresh Thyme	61
Hungarian Cherry Soup	43	Sandy Cake	75
Italian Breakfast Frittata	16	Sardine Fish Cakes	59
Italian Cucumber Salad	65	Saucy Fish Dill	59
Jeweled Cookies	79	Sautéed Green Beans	33
Lemon Cake	80	Sautéed Spicy Cabbage	71
Lemon Chicken & Avocado Salad	25	Shrimp in Garlic Sauce	62
Lentil and Vegetable Soup	91	Shrimp Quesadilla	30
Mango and Pear Smoothie	19	Simple Cabbage Soup	48
Mango Cucumber Salsa	23	Small Chocolate Cakes	76
Mango Lassi Smoothie	19	Soup with Leek, Spinach, and Chicken	43
Marinated Berries	23	Spanish Rice	35
Marinated Shrimp Pasta Salad	34	Spiced Honey Salmon	60
Mediterranean Vegetable Soup	44	Spicy Chicken Soup	47
Mint Zucchini	69	Spicy Crab Dip	25
Minty Cherry Smoothie	21	Spicy Guacamole	73
Minty Olives Salad	69	Spicy Lamb Curry	53
Mixed Berry Cobbler	74	Spinach And Crab Soup	31
Mixed Fruit Salad with Mint-Lime Dressing	101	Spinach and Mushroom Frittata	12
Nutmeg Chicken Soup	42	Spritz Cookies	78
Oatmeal Raisin Cookies	99	Squash and Cranberries	66
Oatmeal with Apples and Cinnamon	83	Squash and Turmeric Soup	45
Omelet with Feta and Fresh Mint	18	Steamed Fish with Garlic	62
Open-Faced Beef Stir-Up	55	Strawberry Muesli	18
Oregon Tuna Patties	63	Strawberry Pie	76
Oven-Fried Southern Style Catfish	59	Strawberry Tiramisu	75
Oven-Roasted Zucchini With Herbs	36	Strengthening Smoothie Bowl	19
Pad Thai	33	Stuffed Sweet Potatoes	88
Panzanella Salad	66	Sweet And Spicy Tortilla Chips	71
Paprika Pork Soup	46	Sweet Potato Toast	85
Peanut Butter Energy Balls	99	Sweet Raspberry Candy	78
Peppercorn Pork Chops	54	Sweet Savory Meatballs	72
Pineapple Bread	17	Teriyaki Beef Skewers	53
Pineapple Cake	77	Thai Chicken Soup	46
Pineapple Smoothie	20	Thai Spiced Halibut	37
Pinna Colada Protein Shake	22	The Kale and Green Lettuce Soup	40
Poached Halibut In Mango Sauce	58	Traditional Black Bean Chili	31
Popcorn With Sugar And Spice	24	Tuna Casserole	38
Pork Loins with Leeks	55	Tuna Macaroni Salad	35
Pork Tenderloin with Roasted Fruit	53	Turkey Broccoli Salad	30
Power-Boosting Smoothie	21	Vanilla Bean Panna Cotta	100
Pumpkin, Coconut and Sage Soup	45	Vegan Blueberry Muffins	85
Quinoa and Vegetable Stir-Fry	95	Vegan Breakfast Burrito	84
Quinoa Salad with Lemon-Dijon Dressing	92	Vegan Breakfast Couscous	86
Quinoa-Stuffed Bell Peppers	91	Vegan Breakfast Quinoa Bars	84
Raspberry Peach Shake	22	Vegan Breakfast Quinoa Salad	84
Raspberry Peach Smoothie	21	Vegan Breakfast Tofu Stir-Fry	87

Made in the USA
Coppell, TX
15 September 2024

37291360R00063